"*The Road to Pelican* was an inspi
teling has woven a fascinating narrative that is a delight to read. The way the
author traces the threads of the past while walking in her ancestors' footsteps
helped to ground the story in the larger state and nation-wide context, while
still maintaining a heartfelt, personal and relevant feeling. I recommend this
book for anyone interested in history, genealogy and for those looking for the
inspiration to dig deeper into their own pasts."

—**Beth Wemigwase**, Program Coordinator,
Harbor Springs Area Historical Society

"Marla Kay Houghteling's *The Road to Pelican* traces the parallel journeys of
her pioneer great grandmother in the 1870s and her own wanderings, a century later. This is a fascinating and detailed account, brimming in the history
of 19th century Wisconsin and Minnesota. *The Road to Pelican* works effec-
tively as a carefully researched historical document with a wealth of primary
sources. It is also the personal memoir of a writer with deep attachment to
the storied, natural world. Readers will delight in Houghteling's insightful
and often humorous observations, and—upon reading the final page—agree
that she has '[left] behind a legacy as valuable' as that of her pioneer family."

—**Linda S. De La Ysla**, MFA, MS, Ph.D. Associate Professor (retired),
English Dept. Community College of Baltimore County,
author of "Faculty as First Responders: Willing but Unprepared"
in *Generation Vet: Composition, Student-Veterans,
and the Post-9/11 University*

"This book is a vivid and introspective account of parallel journeys—that
of Houghteling's great-grandmother Sarah from Wisconsin to Minnesota
in the early 1870s, and Houghteling's retracing of that journey more than
100 years later. Overlaid on these physical journeys are both women's emotional voyages. Houghteling interweaves well-chosen excerpts from Sarah's
journal and other historical sources with her own lyrical prose, producing a
narrative that honors the past while connecting it to the present. An accom-
plished poet, Houghteling's prose is tight and quick-moving, painting both
her great-grandmother's journey and her own in vivid hues. The reader
emerges with a deeper understanding of 1870s pioneer living, including

house-building, child-rearing, unexpected joys and tragedies, and family ties both strained and strengthened. Houghteling adeptly places her own journey to rural northern Michigan and a new marriage alongside the travels of her great-grandmother, a juxtaposition that enriches both stories and underscores the timelessness of our quest to find meaning within ourselves, between one another, and in connection with the natural world."

—**Dr. Mark Blaauw-Hara**, Assistant Professor, Teaching Stream, Institute for the Study of University Pedagogy, University of Toronto Mississauga

"In *The Road to Pelican* by Marla Kay Houghteling, we follow the author's journey to retrace her family's historic path as they emigrated from Wisconsin to Minnesota in 1871. This meticulously researched book follows Houghteling's great grandmother, Sarah Moore Leonard Cole, and some of her close family, as they made this long and arduous trip to their new home. Interspersed with this historical story is the author's account of her own transplantation as an adult, and the ways it mirrored her ancestors. The strength of familial bonds, the act of carrying these bonds on through the act of writing (Sarah's poetry of her life and journey), carry throughout this remarkable book."

—**Mary Beauchamp**, Reference/Collection Development Librarian, Petoskey District Library

# *The* ROAD TO PELICAN

## MARLA KAY HOUGHTELING

MISSION POINT PRESS

Author's Note:
*Though this book is being published in 2022, it was researched and written*
*during 1997 to 2000. Much has changed on the American scene since then.*
*The author invites the reader to travel that road with her*
*before the advent of the 21st century.*

Published by Mission Point Press
2554 Chandler Rd.
Traverse City, MI 49696
(231) 421-9513
www.MissionPointPress.com

ISBN: 978-1-958363-31-7
LOC: 2022915497

Printed in the United States of America

*For Norm—*
*and so the journey continues*

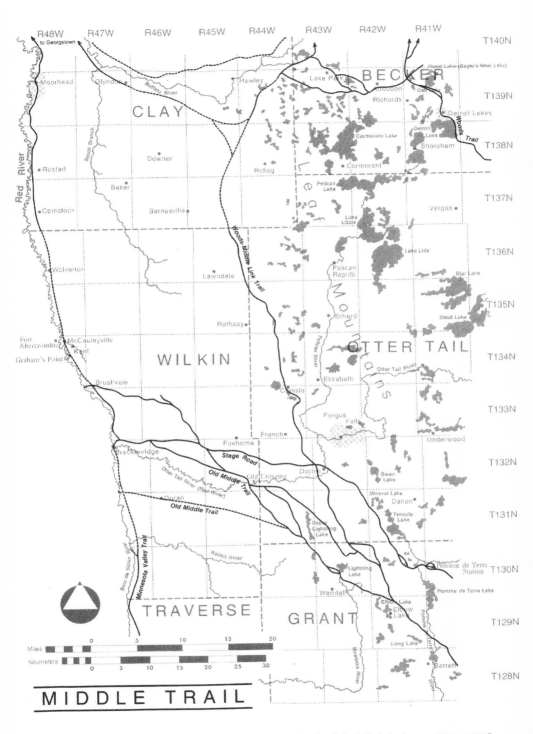

*Map from "The Red River Trails—Oxcart Routes Between St. Paul and the Selkirk Settlement 1820–1870" by Rhoda R. Gilman, Carolyn Gilman, and Deborah M. Stultz, 1979. Courtesy of Minnesota Historical Society, Gale Family Library.pdf*

# CONTENTS

Preface                                                                    xi

Why I Am Here: June 19, 1998                                               xv

THE BUBBLE BURSTS                                                           1

Lemonweir Valley, Wisconsin 1868                                           1

Chester County, Pennsylvania 1992                                          7

MINNESOTA FEVER                                                            11

Lone Rock Farm, 1871                                                       11

Malvern, Pennsylvania March 1996                                          15

PICKING UP THE TRAIL                                                      17

Mauston, Wisconsin May 19–21, 1997                                        17

BIG CITY LIGHTS                                                           27

Lone Rock to St. Paul: Two Weeks, April, May 1871                         27

Lone Rock to St. Paul: Seven-and-a-half

   Hours (Including a stop in Tomah) June 1998               30

RED RIVER TRAILS                                                          41

May 1871                                                                  41

June 19, 1998                                                             43

PELICAN RAPIDS, THEN AND NOW                                             47

June 6, 1871                                                             47

June 19 and 20, 1998                                                     50

CAMPING OUT—AND FOOD                                                      59

Summer 1871                                                              59

Camping in My Life                                                       61

AMONG THE DEAD                                                           65

June 21, 1998                                                            65

PLATES                                              71 — 78

THE RIGHT SPOT                                            79
*June 1871*                                               79
*June 21, 1998*                                           79

TILLIE'S STORY                                           83
*June 22, 1998*                                          83

LIVING IN THE WAGONS                                    89
*Summer 1871*                                           89
*Summer 1998, post-Pelican*                             92

BUILDING THE HOUSE                                      97
*Early fall 1871*                                        97
*Late summer through remainder of 1998*                 98

SETTLING IN                                            103
*1872, 1873*                                           103
*Summer 1999*                                          107

INDIANS—A DISMAL TUNE                                  111
*1870s—after New Ulm*                                  111

BECOMING A LOCAL                                       115
*1875*                                                 115
*1999*                                                 117

A PROGRESSIVE WORLD                                    119
*1889–1902*                                            119

A BETTER COUNTRY                                       127

*About the Author*                                     131
*Endnotes*                                             132
*Bibliography*                                         134
*Acknowledgments*                                      136

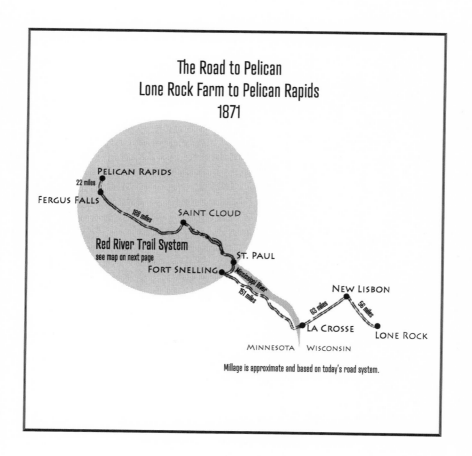

The Road to Pelican
Lone Rock Farm to Pelican Rapids
1871

# PREFACE

A piece of writing is a powerful legacy, more precious than antique furniture or silver.

I'm fortunate to have a copy of my great-grandmother's account of her family's emigration from Wisconsin to Minnesota in 1871. I also have letters written by her children, especially by Georgina, the "baby in the wagon." My great-grandmother, Sarah Moore Leonard Cole, did not keep a diary during her original journey, but wrote about the experience later in her life. The piece was published in an edited version in the *St. Paul Farmers' Dispatch* in 1915.

I was born over one hundred years after my maternal great-grandmother, but I felt connected to her because she had cared enough to record her experiences. Many families had followed the Red River Trails that scratched their way across Minnesota. Some had more harrowing experiences; some continued on west, into greater unknown. But not all wrote of their lives, or if they did, not all writing survived. I am grateful to family members who took care to see her words were passed on. In interacting with her writing, I experienced a powerful tug from family and land.

I had known for several years I had to retrace the wagon route of 1871. I planned to do it in my Toyota Camry by myself, perhaps with my dog. At that time, I was divorced and living several states away from my relatives. But I, like Sarah, decided to move, from Pennsylvania to Michigan, where I had been born and raised. Geographically closer, I also grew emotionally closer to my mother, my two sisters, and their families.

I made the first exploration on my own in May of 1997. I drove to Mauston, Wisconsin, to see for myself the Lemonweir Valley and to start to put together Sarah's emigration. My mother met me there on her way to Canada to visit her eldest sister. The following year, my new husband and I drove from northern Michigan to Mauston and took the wagon trail to Pelican Rapids, Minnesota.

I embarked on writing this book while beginning another more intimate adventure—a second marriage. Five years after a divorce, I had regained my emotional stability. My new husband was ready for another marriage after the death of his first wife in 1995. Norm and I met "in a happy coincidence," after we had both moved to Michigan's "tip of the mitt." At our first meeting, we discovered we had lived for twenty-five years in the same area in Pennsylvania, within five miles of each other.

Even after our marriage, I considered making the trip alone. It was *my* project. But in rereading Sarah's account and old letters of the Cole family, I realized this was not meant to be a solo trip. Sarah had not made the trip alone. She had been surrounded by family. Three wagons rolled out of Lone Rock Farm, outside Mauston, Wisconsin. Her whole adventure and life were a family project. Following her trail and seeing the area that had drawn her reconnected me with my family. It gave me an appreciation for those who are living and the importance of family ties.

While I was writing this book, President Clinton was impeached by the House and standing trial in the Senate. The fact that the Coles had been witnesses to the only other impeachment gave me one more connection to my ancestors. As that trial began on March 23, 1868, it's a good bet that Sarah and her family were in favor of Andrew Johnson's removal from office. His reconstruction policies were not popular with northerners. As farmers in Wisconsin's Lemonweir Valley, they were experiencing a boom in the market for hops only three years after the Civil War ended. President Johnson's leniency toward the former Confederate states could have been seen as a threat toward their post-war prosperity.

Another parallel experience was that of homesteading. In September of 1998, my husband and I began construction of our white cedar house on ten acres. With each step, I compared our experiences with those of the Coles in clearing timberland and putting up a house in 1871. Our project took much longer.

While living with *The Road to Pelican*, my ears and eyes became magnets for any references to the 1870s. Suddenly the radio, magazines, and books seemed full of events coinciding with the first years of Sarah's marriage:

1869 Frank Lloyd Wright born in Richland Center, Wisconsin

1870 Irrigation came to Greeley, Colorado

1870 Cape Hatteras Lighthouse built

1870 August Lindbergh, father of Charles Lindbergh, became an American citizen, after moving to Minnesota from Sweden

1870 Sophia Smith signed her will, which founded Smith College for women

1871 Paul Verlaine and Arthur Rimbaud met

1871 Livingstone found by Stanley

1871 Chicago and Peshtigo fires

1872 U.S. Weather Bureau sent up first balloon

1872 Susan B. Anthony arrested in Rochester, New York, for trying to vote

1872 First Arbor Day

The only events within the radius of the Coles' awareness were the Chicago and Peshtigo fires. No doubt, they received news from their relatives back in Wisconsin of the fires' devastation, but in October of 1871, they were consumed with getting ready for their first Minnesota winter.

# WHY I AM HERE

## *June 19, 1998*

At almost fifty-two, I am caught up with the idea of following great-grandmother and her family in their wagons, even though it is 127 years later. I have faith that there will be clues, if not physical, then psychic or spiritual. And not just clues about their journey, but clues about my own. I've become more and more convinced that I was meant to make this trip.

I'm traveling with my husband of six months (this is a second marriage for both of us); we are thriving on the freedom from daily responsibilities and the excitement of the unknown ahead of us. As we piece together the Wisconsin to Minnesota trip, my great-grandmother, Sarah Moore Leonard Cole, is always just a bit ahead of us.

I suspect the name *Lemonweir* may have been an initial factor in luring me here. When I read my great-grandmother's account and first heard of the Lemonweir Valley in Wisconsin, I wanted to know more. That name had a siren-like quality and pricked my dormant sense of adventure. I imagined a slim, green river like one in old English folk songs winding through lemon groves. I wanted to know why she, a young married woman with a baby, would leave such an idyllic-sounding place and move to Minnesota, without knowing exactly where or how they would live. I was attracted to the journey of this woman I had never known; I wanted to see if I felt any connection, any "familial memory." I'd gone through much of my adulthood thinking I could live as if family origins had no real bearing on me. As I approached my fiftieth birthday, I started looking for a definition of who I was in relation to previous generations.

Underlying all these explanations is the bottom line of any journey. As Frank McCourt writes in *'Tis* about his trip back to Ireland to attend the funeral of his father from whom he had been estranged for years: *I flew to my father's funeral in Belfast in the hope I might discover why I was flying to my father's funeral in Belfast.* This is true of me; I'm retracing Sarah Cole's wagon route in order to find out why I'm retracing Sarah Cole's wagon route.

# THE BUBBLE BURSTS

## Lemonweir Valley, Wisconsin 1868

*There had been a great boom in hop-raising among many of the farmers in that vicinity, when suddenly the market was o verstocked and the bubble burst. Many were nearly wricked [sic] with debt, my husband's father being one of the unfortunate ones. It was a sad and anxious time for us all.*
—Sarah Moore Leonard Cole

The Coles, the family Sarah Moore Leonard married into, raised hops, a member of the hemp family Cannabaceae and an essential ingredient in beer-making; it gave a slightly bitter taste to the too-sweet, fermented beverage. It was also discovered that adding hops helped prolong the quality of beer. In her lifetime, Sarah did not drink beer or alcohol in any form.

During and right after the Civil War was a boom time for the Wisconsin hops growers. The hops louse was responsible for this prosperity. When the insect devastated crops in New York and other eastern states, Wisconsin, which had always raised some hops, threw itself wholeheartedly into hops growing. The price went from 15¢ a pound in 1861, to 65¢ in 1865, and after the war it rose to 72¢. Profits were ranging from $800 to $1200 an acre during the war.[1] Sauk County was the center of hops growing, but the crop soon spread to other counties, including Juneau in central Wisconsin, where the Coles and Leonards farmed.

The hops plant produces vines yards long, which lengthen as much as six inches a day during the growing season. When the cone-shaped, deep yellow flowers bloom from the silvery green bud, they are picked and dried. The best-tasting hops come from flowers picked when small with thin leaves.

Growing hops was an involved process; it was a crop one didn't take on lightly. The book published for Juneau County's centennial gives some insight into the work involved:

*The vines would grow in both light and heavy soil and would tolerate moderately dry weather. Roots were planted each spring in hills eight feet apart with eight feet between rows. When the first shoots appeared three ten-to-fifteen foot long willow poles were put firmly into the ground at each hill. The vines twined around each pole and were tied on with yarn each day. The poles were tied together at the top and the vines intertwined there.*

*When the hops turned a yellowish-green, they were ready for harvest. Hop yards were set up near the hop houses and the poles loaded with vines and hops were loaded on long wagons with a sort of fence down the middle against which the poles were placed. At the hop yard men used a hop knife to cut the vines and separate the poles before leaning them against the hop rack. The picker stood or sat between the piles of poles and picked the hops. A coarse burlap bag—'hopsack' material—able to hold several bushels of hops was hung open in front of the picker. A good picker would pick fifty or sixty bushels of hops per day.*

In 1868, Sarah Moore Leonard married George Washington Cole. She was twenty-three years old and, until she married, lived with her father, stepmother, and brother. The Leonard family had emigrated from Maine to Wisconsin in 1859. Sarah was only six when her mother died and her father's second wife "duly spanked and took good care of her but never really loved her."[2] At sixteen, she took on her first teaching job, which would launch her into a lifelong career. What brought the Leonards to Wisconsin is not known. Once there, Evander Leonard, Sarah's father, did not throw himself into hops raising.

However, the Coles did. Her in-laws, Levi and Hannah Cole, had come from Troy, New York, in 1844. They first settled near Lyon in Walworth County on the southern border, where her future husband, George Washington Cole, was born in 1846. Four years later, the senior Coles moved to Lindina, near Lone Rock, southwest of Maughs Mills, now called Mauston, in Juneau County, in the southwestern region of the state.

2

The Coles experienced the transition of Wisconsin from a territory to a state in 1848. Since they were living in Walworth County for several years, they also experienced the "reign" of King Strang. James Jesse Strang, also originally from New York State, was pretender to the throne of Mormon leadership. After Joseph Smith's shooting death in 1844, Strang, who was practicing law at that time, urged the Mormons of the Nauvoo settlement in Illinois to follow him to a refuge in Wisconsin. He claimed to have received a letter from Smith, dated the day before Smith's death, instructing him to build a temple and city in Walworth County. Some joined up with Strang and temple building commenced. Under Strang's direction, diggers "discovered" metal plates with mysterious markings buried in a casket under an old oak tree. Strang's claim that these "plates of Laban," giving him the authority to lead the Mormons, was a direct challenge to Brigham Young. By 1847 he decided to establish an empire on Beaver Island in Lake Michigan. He began moving the faithful to the isolated spot, which proved to be the site of his own murder. He was assassinated by his own followers, a pair of disenchanted "Saints." Perhaps the temple-building neighbors in Walworth County precipitated the Coles' move to Juneau County.

Sarah and George married in a year when Juneau County was "crazy for hops." In 1868 Juneau County saw its biggest year. Mauston, the town nearest their homestead, shipped out $30,000 worth of hops in one day and over $400,000 for the season. Many farmers had planted every available acre with hops, and they went into debt to mortgage more farmland. There was a wave of conspicuous consumption, with formerly frugal farmers buying fancy buggies, furniture, and clothes. Accounts from the boom years speak of "farmers' daughters … in silks and satins," purchasing pianos and visiting foreign courts, while the farmers' sons "changed overalls for broadcloth and sported blooded horses and fancy phaetons."[3]

The book published for the centennial gives a detailed account of the days of the "hops rush."

*In the boom days, hops-pickers—usually young women—were recruited in the cities and traveled by rail to the country at harvest time. The work was tolerable and growers could afford to pay large number of harvesters. After the boom, pick-*

*ing hops became a chore for Winnebago women. They brought their babies along tightly-bound in skin-covered cradle-boards. The boards, with babies still inside, were hung on the hop rack so mother and child were never out of each other's sight. The Indians were inveterate tobacco chewers in those days and the men working with them all marvelled at the women's ability to spit a wad all the way over the top of the rack.*

*[T]he hop house ... was a tightly-built two-story shed with a large furnace at one end, 'an immense affair, capable of receiving ordinary cord-wood, and as a high temperature must be constantly maintained ... is constructed without espe-cial reference to economy in fuel.'*

*Green hops were spread out on the second floor of the hop shed, and the fire lit. Sulfur or 'brimstone,' as it was called was also burned in the furnace room so its fumes would 'bleach out the rusty spots on the leaves.' Clouds of steam from the drying hops slipped through vents at the eaves or out a cupola on the roof. When dry the hops were raked out of the drying room to a store room until they were ready to be shipped.*

Since the Coles ended up with big debts after the crash of the Wisconsin hops market, they must have invested heavily. Did they use pickers in their fields? Or did the families work together? Levi Cole Sr. and his wife Hannah Van Arnam Cole had three sons and two daughters. Perhaps they did some of their own picking and hired some of the young women who came by rail. An account from the *Wisconsin State Register* tells of a gold rush-like atmosphere that engulfed the Wisconsin counties:

*Far and near from the surrounding country girls and women of every class and condition, in response to the call for pickers, streamed into the hop gardens. 'The railroad companies are utterly unable to furnish cars for the accommodation of the countless throngs who daily find their way to the depots ... to take the cars for the hop fields. Every passenger car is pressed into service, and freight and platform cars are fixed up as well as possible for the transportation of the pickers. Every train has the appearance of an excursion train, on some great gala day, loaded down as they are with myriads of bright-faced, young girls ...'*

*The girls, in addition to receiving their board, were ordinarily paid at the rate of 50 cents per ten-pound box, a rate which permitted industrious workers to earn*

4

*readily from $1.75 to $2.25 a day. … The picking season was a time of feasting*
*and merrymaking. Each night when darkness put an end to labor, the well-used*
*fiddle was fetched from its case, and to its merry strains, under the mellow autumn*
*moon the unwearied tripped the jovial steps of the hop dance.*[4]

The golden days of hops in Juneau County were waning in 1869, and the
boom had ended by 1870. Things had improved out east. The farmers there
had managed to banish the hops louse and produce bumper crops, thus
flooding the market. Wisconsin hops growers felt this glut as yields were cut
by almost 50 percent.[5] Even worse was the arrival of the hops louse, which
had migrated west. The price of hops fell to as low as 34 a pound. The whole
economy was affected. Farmers went bust as well as those who had linked
their fortunes to the fields: bankers, merchants, tradesmen.

Somehow Levi Cole Sr. and his oldest son, William Henry Cole, held on
until 1871. Sarah writes of the Cole land in the Lemonweir Valley:

*We were married in Sept. 1868 with little to start a family life beside good health,*
*love and optimistic views for the future. My husband's parents were early pioneers*
*in the Lemonweir valley in Wisconsin (about 1850), who took a 160 acre home-*
*stead. They were honest, pious, hard-working people, and their pioneer experi-*
*ences were very much more severe than ours of later date, though very interesting*
*to us in the telling; Indians were plenty and all resources primitive. Their main*
*object seemed to be to locate their three sons on this land when they arrived at*
*maturity, giving each a 'forty' and having the old home on the fourth, to keep the*
*family from ever being separated. There were two daughters, but as a matter of*
*course they would go to a home with a husband.*

Sarah must have relished entering this large Cole clan. She seems eager to
join into family life. Perhaps losing her mother at an early age, and the small
size of the Leonard household, produced a longing to be part of a full-size
family. The Coles seemed close-knit, which makes it a bit disturbing to realize that soon most of the family would vacate their lovely spot in the Lemonweir Valley, even the elders who had already had one pioneering experience
decades before and were now forced to make another one. This time they'd
have the support of their children.

Any myths about families in the nineteenth century being more geographically stable, being born and dying in the same house or even bed, are dispelled by the Coles' moves across the country. There must have been something about life in Wisconsin that attracted Levi and Hannah Cole enough to make them pull up roots and leave New York State. The 1840s in New York's Hudson River Valley were times of protest and a growing Anti-Renter movement. Farmers paid rent and taxes on land owned by mostly Dutch landlords, a system perpetuated since the "patroonship" of the 1600s. Perhaps the Coles were looking for a place where they could own their own land and share it with their children. They may have been among the thousands of renter-farmers oppressed by a feudal system in a country based on individual freedoms. Wisconsin may have held the promise of achieving some economic autonomy.

However, this theory was dispelled when I came across a letter written by George's daughter. She told that Levi had owned a supply store for canal boat owners on the Erie Canal. Levi had been taken by his father, Eddy Cole, to see Lafayette in 1824 when the famous general visited New York and rode up the canal on a packet boat, before the canal was officially finished in 1825. So Levi, for reasons unknown, had switched from canal to fields.

Levi and Hannah's farm in the Lemonweir Valley was near Lone Rock. There was, and still is, a tall rocky structure jutting up unexpectedly from the farm soil. It's one of those quirks of geology that makes Wisconsin's topography constantly surprising. Although Sarah and George were a part of the clan, they also wanted to claim some autonomy from the Cole elders. The young couple did not live on his parents' farm during the three years of married life in Wisconsin. Sarah writes:

> *Their plan for the sons worked well with the two older ones, but the youngest was inclined to agree with me in wishing to strike out for ourselves. So as I had chosen a humble life and could realize I must play other instruments that would spoil piano playing, I sold the piano I had paid for by teaching and invested it toward building and furnishing a little home on an undivided half of my brother's farm. We had some help from my father and were getting along very nicely ...*

As young marrieds, Sarah and George lived on Leonard land, rather than on the Cole farm. She did so at a cost, selling her piano. Lindina, the area where Lone Rock reared up, was the first town to have more than one thousand cattle and the first to have more than ten pianos.[6] Having a piano in the parlor was a mark of culture, so Sarah's decision to sell the piano, which she had bought with teaching money, must have been a difficult one. This funding of the new house with piano money is reported dispassionately by her, but it was a significant sacrifice. Hard physical labor was part of a teacher's job description. She had earned her piano money by building fires in the stove, perhaps even chopping her own wood, sweeping away dirt inside, and clearing snow and mud outside the schoolhouse.

After hops disappeared from the scene, wheat became the big crop of Wisconsin in the second half of the 1800s. One wonders why the Coles didn't turn to wheat farming after the bubble burst.

## Chester County, Pennsylvania 1992

There was nothing to keep me in Pennsylvania. Several friends had moved away; one dear friend had died. My husband and I were separated, a divorce pending. I was unhappy in my job. The steady paycheck was the only advantage, but the company could be sold at any time, and my job could disappear. Suddenly the town in which I'd lived for twenty-five years seemed to have no hold on me. There would be sadness in leaving friends and familiar routines, but it was outweighed by the excitement of leaving, of making a change. I'd spent most of my adult life away from my parents and sisters, aunts, uncles, and now nieces and a nephew. Seeing them only once a year, or every two years, was no longer sufficient. I wanted more of a connection, more physical proximity.

I grew up in western Michigan. During my Pennsylvania years, I had yearned for sand dunes and pines. Whenever I returned for family visits, I headed for Lake Michigan, no matter the season. I had to be near water. As my great-uncle Maurice told me when I was home for Thanksgiving, just a year before my husband and I separated, "You've got to live by water." For him, there was simply no other location. I knew he was right. I was parched, emotionally and spiritually. The promise of water was comforting. Water would heal and renew me.

It was around this time that I began rereading Sarah's account with the idea of retracing her route. An edited version had been published on June 11, 1915, in the *St. Paul Farmers' Dispatch* as the winning entry in a contest calling for pioneering experiences. A typewritten copy of the unedited version had been given to me fifteen years before by my Aunt Beth, my mother's older sister, who was the keeper of many Cole family mementos. The copy I received was five pages of single-spaced typing, with a copy of the letter from the editor sent to Sarah Cole. The newspaper had requested pioneer stories, with $5 going to the first-place account:

*Farmers' Dispatch*
*St. Paul, Minn.*
*July 2, 1915*
*Mrs. Geo. W. Cole,*
*Pelican Rapids, Minn.*
*Dear Madam:*
*I am herewith sending you [a] check for $5.25, same being payment for the personal experience story written by you and published in the Farmers' Dispatch during the month of June.*

*May I take this occasion to express our appreciation for the interest you have shown. The story was satisfactory in every way and I am glad to have been in [a] position to accept it.*

*Very truly yours,*
*Farmers' Dispatch*
*(Signed) S.E. Elliott (Editor)*

Since that typewritten copy, other copies from various cardboard boxes stored by Coles have come my way. One had some comments attached by Georgina Cole, Sarah's oldest daughter, the baby who made the trip in the wagon from Wisconsin to Minnesota. I kept these papers, along with old family letters and pictures passed on by my mother and aunts, in a wicker creel. I retyped Sarah's account over the years to renew my acquaintance with it. In my pre-computer days, with the aid of correcto-tape, I used an old Royal typewriter; then around 1981, on a Commodore computer; the mid-'80s and into the '90s on several IBM-compatible computers; and most recently on my Compaq laptop.

Back in 1988, after ten years of contributing essays and poems to *The Christian Science Monitor,* two poems and an accompanying short essay inspired by Sarah were published in the newspaper. I had taken the first step in interacting publicly with her material.

★   ★   ★

## Minnesota Fever
*(Impressions from the memoirs of Sarah Leonard Cole, 1871)*

*The piano is sold, the wagon filled*
*With all we own. Wisconsin is behind*
*Us now in the tall grasses of April.*

*Our little French pony seems not to mind*
*Ducks and hens, the cows' meditative pace.*
*We camp where trees sway and the stars are kind.*

*With my apron I cover baby's face,*
*For the mosquitoes are anxious to feed.*
*The Pomme de Terre is banked with Queen Anne's lace.*

*One keg of soap; bushel of early-rose seed;*
*Thirty-five yards of rag rug; butter churn;*
*Wedding chest. An answer for every need.*

*With Minnesota fever our hearts burn.*
*We'll fish, plant, gather as the seasons turn.*
*What the prairie will teach us we can learn.*

In 1988 I had not yet seen the banks of the Pomme de Terre, and when I did finally see the river, there was no Queen Anne's lace; the banks were reedy and marshy. Sarah's references to mosquitoes are to the ones she contended with at their homestead site. I sacrificed details for the rhyme scheme. Even as I wrote the poems, I knew I had started a journey; I had joined the wagons.

Sarah's optimism and sense of adventure shine through the dated prose and long sentences. During those years when I felt my life was at a standstill or I was in limbo, I'd retrieve the pages and read about "Carving a Home Out of the Wilderness," her title for the account. (The newspaper titled the piece "Trials of Homesteading—A Woman Tells of Cutting a Home in Timber Land.")

When my marriage had officially ended, the house where I'd lived for sixteen years empty of all my possessions and the key turned over to new owners, I was ready for an adventure. Finally in 1996, at the age of forty-nine, I made the break and moved to northern Michigan. A journey from southeastern Pennsylvania to Michigan's "tip of the mitt" does not have epic proportions, but I felt as though I were climbing Mt. Everest. It isn't necessary to travel to another continent to have an adventure or to change your life.

# MINNESOTA FEVER

## *Lone Rock Farm, 1871*

*One afternoon in April we went to visit the eldest son and found them all fired up with plans to emigrate to Minnesota. They had received literature from Frazee City praising the country in the highest terms, and as some changes must be made, the father and eldest son had decided to sell their homes to be freed from debt and start anew. Of course they were very enthusiastic and we talked of little else. When we were on the way home, my husband after a long silence said to me: 'How would you like to go to Minnesota?' That was just what I wanted to hear, and I said, 'I'd just love to.' 'Well then,' said he, 'we'll go.'*

*When my father heard of our plans he made it his business to 'put a stop to such foolishness.' The idea of giving up a good start, to go off among the Indians and all sorts of hardships! I was not to think of such a thing! But we had the Minnesota fever hard; go we would, and go we did.*

—Sarah Moore Leonard Cole

Sarah and George were young marrieds with a baby. They were at a critical point: they could stay and establish their family in the Lemonweir Valley—or they could head west and forge new opportunities. The literature from Frazee City was enticing. They would be emigrating with family; there was comfort in knowing they would not be making the leap alone.

Not everyone had come down with Minnesota fever. Sarah's father, Evander Leonard, and her brother, Melvin Leonard, would not emigrate in 1871. And Levi Cole's middle son, Levi Jr., remained in the Lemonweir Valley, keeping the farm for several more decades. Levi Cole Sr. had a brother Elias, who also had settled in Wisconsin. He remained there.

Three wagons pulled out of Lone Rock Farm on April 27, 1871. Sarah, George, and their baby daughter, Georgina, were in one wagon. The eldest son, William Henry, his wife, Mary Elizabeth Cady, and their five children (two girls and three boys) filled the second wagon. This couple would have a total of eight children during their marriage. The third carried the elders, Levi Cole and Hannah Van Arnam Cole. Now in their sixties, they were pioneers again.

Just two years before her death in 1943, Georgina Cole Harris, the baby in the wagon, wrote a letter to her brother Daniel Cole. Georgina was a faithful and prolific letter writer. From Tacoma, Washington, where she was living then and recovering from a stroke, she wrote:

> I am glad Grace and Kathleen had a chance to see Lone Rock and the place where I was born. George took me out there more than once, and we found the very house where I was born, and the schoolhouse where mama taught right up to within two months of the time I was born!

Since Sarah reports that they did not live on the farm with the elder Coles, Georgina's letter is confusing. How could she have been born at Lone Rock if her parents were living on Leonard land? Perhaps Sarah went to Lone Rock to be taken care of when she gave birth. Perhaps the Leonard farm adjoined Cole property and the whole area was referred to as Lone Rock.

Levi Jr., the middle son, stayed at Lone Rock while most of his relatives headed west. He farmed there until 1897 when he retired and moved into the town of Mauston. In 1865 he married Frances Risdon, born in England, with whom he had three children. The rest of the family was busy packing up. Sarah tells of the rather impulsive pulling up of stakes:

> In two weeks time from the birth of the idea we had disposed of what we could not take with us, (which was little beside our house and share in the farm, the latter not being paid for and my brother released us from the debt by taking it back), and we were on the road. We had a good team of horses, a good covered emigrant wagon or 'prairie schooner,' a nice little French pony, a great pet named Jockey,

*two cows and some hens and ducks in coops at the sides of our wagon, which was well loaded, for I think we took everything we had in the house except stove, table and dining chairs.*

*I packed my bureau (or large chest of drawers given me by my father as a wedding present) with dry goods, and we laid it on its back in the bottom of the wagon. I had 35 yards of new rag carpeting which, on top of the bureau and other things, made a comfortable foundation for a bed. My dishes were packed in a barrel. It was surprising what went into that wagon, even a keg of 'soft soap' and a bushel of 'early rose' seed potatoes, a high chair for our baby, and an old-fashioned splint-bottom rocking chair which father had also given me, and a chair for my husband; so we each had a chair.*

What a feeling of freedom, to have all earthly possessions in one small space, and to have everything that was needed. The thought is exhilarating. However, the periodic uprooting of a settled piece of land may not have been exhilarating to them. My ancestors seemed to move a lot. It rather dispels the notion of the stable, solid nineteenth century life, where the old homestead was passed on to succeeding generations. The younger Coles may have seen the move as an adventure, but the older people were not packing up for something exciting to do. Economics kept them unsettled. Sarah continues:

*We will never forget our starting away from the old home, for it was heart rending, not so much for us young people, but the old people to leave a home that they had taken from the wilderness and made it one of the finest places in the whole valley, with a beautiful orchard, some of the fruit trees having been grown from seed, not to mention the old pioneer friends and relatives. We made quite a spectacle too, with our three covered wagons and a small herd of cattle, one of the men riding the Kanuck pony and driving the cattle. We started as soon as the grass would feed the cattle on the way, which was April 27, 1871.*

The prairie schooner was named for the arched white canvas covering which resembled the sails of a ship. It was similar to the Conestoga wagon, used during the early 1800s in the east to transport freight. The prairie schooner was lighter and could be drawn by as few as two horses, as compared to the six-horse teams needed for the Conestoga. A farm wagon could be converted

13

to a prairie schooner by attaching horseshoe-shaped wooden arches and covering them with canvas, leaving oval-shaped openings at both ends.

As the Coles "set sail," they were leaving a state that was moving ahead during the turbulent years of Reconstruction. President Andrew Johnson was seen as being soft on the South. He had vetoed the Freedmen's Bureau Act and the Civil Rights Act, Reconstruction laws passed by the Republican Congress. The dissatisfaction with the chief executive culminated in an impeachment trial. In 1870, Wisconsin senator James R. Doolittle's term expired, and he was out. He had chosen the unpopular path of supporting Johnson, going against the wishes of his constituency. The Wisconsin legislature had adopted resolutions instructing him to resign, but he ignored them.

Moving toward a more inclusive society, Wisconsin had ratified the Fifteenth Amendment in 1869, guaranteeing people of color, which included former slaves, the right to vote. And in 1871, the legislature had enacted to add a college for women to the State University.

Another event in 1871 became more famous and left a dark cloud over Wisconsin. On October 8, the Great Fire engulfed a third of Chicago. Thousands of new residents were living in wooden "balloon frame" houses, invented in the 1830s.[7] Three hundred died. However, on the same night, Peshtigo, Wisconsin, a town which had supplied much of the house-building lumber for Chicago, also burned. When the inferno ended, only one house, still in the process of being built, stood.

There had been a drought in northern Wisconsin since July 8. Wells dried up, swamps disappeared, and streams stopped flowing. The fences in the fields were long lines of ashes. "A pall of smoke overhung the doomed county" from the incessant fires. Breathing was painful in the smoke-laden air of October 8. A hot southerly gale whipped up flames, which pursued fleeing men, women, and children. People jumped into the river to save themselves. The fire spread to sixteen other towns in northeast Wisconsin, killing twelve hundred people.

In October of 1871, on their homestead near Prairie Lake, just outside Pelican Rapids, Minnesota, Sarah and George Cole were moving into their newly built house.

## *Malvern, Pennsylvania March 1996*

I thought about Sarah with envy as I prepared to move to Michigan. How I wished all of my possessions could be packed into a wagon. I was a single woman with a dog and a cat. I was hiring a Bekins truck to haul my furniture, dishes, pots and pans, books, TV, stereo equipment, records, CDs, computer, file cabinets, knickknacks, paintings, photographs, and clothing. I loaded my Toyota with essentials for my rented house in Michigan. I was told the Bekins load would be delivered from two days to a week. I packed every available space in the car with the necessities: the coffeemaker, radio, a box of books and papers, sleeping bag and pillows, a box of kitchen items, pet supplies, the dog in the front on her bed, the cat in the back in her carrier with the litter box beside her.

Unlike Sarah Cole, who had no house awaiting her at the journey's end, I had somewhere to put all my stuff. In January, I'd received an MFA in Writing. I'd made my way from Vermont back down to Pennsylvania in the wake of the Blizzard of '96. The interstates had barely reopened; most exits were slushy, frozen messes, which made stops for gas, food, and restrooms treacherous undertakings. I returned to my office job for three weeks, my resignation effective on Groundhog Day. I drove out to Michigan, dropping off boxes of possessions I didn't trust to professional movers at my sister's place in Whitehall. Then I drove north through blowing snow on slippery county roads. I had sent my resume to two community colleges and planned to look for a place to live somewhere between Traverse City and Petoskey. The receptionist at a Traverse City real estate office told me of a place for rent. I drove out through the white landscape. As I took a turn off the main highway, groups of whitetail deer crossed the road in ballet-like bounds. The house was large with a glimpse of the water, now frozen, through the woods. It felt too isolated, and it was only available until the summer. The second place I looked at was a basement apartment beneath a real estate office. It had rippled brown carpeting and pipes in the ceiling. I was depressed just looking at it.

Some inner magnet pulled me further north to Petoskey. I checked in to the Petoskey Motel, bought a local paper, paid a visit to the chair of the Communications and Humanities (formerly known as English) Department at the community college, and made an appointment to see a house, actually the lower floor of a house. Within twenty-four hours, I had paid a deposit on a two-bedroom house, opened a post office box in Petoskey, and was heading back to Pennsylvania to pack my wagon.

I was loosed from my moorings—bombarded alternately by terror and giddiness, but feeling an underlying calm, an assurance that I would do all right. While still working at my office job, I had cut out a picture from some press materials that had come across my desk. The picture was of a gray-shingled bungalow with a blue door with double windows on each side. A simple wooden deck on the front held a rustic chair and bench, a watering can, pansies, and gladioli. A bank of nasturtiums covered the foreground. There was no water in the picture, but I got the feeling that the house was near a lake or river, perhaps just beyond the nasturtiums.

I would gaze at that picture while rumors of layoffs and department closings swirled around me. When I felt a stress headache coming on, I'd take a deep breath and tell myself, "Soon, soon." I wanted to live in that house.

When I left Pennsylvania for good on March 1, the roads were clear. Gone were all traces of the Blizzard of '96, the January storm that had closed down interstates and isolated cities. I made it across Ohio with no problem. Michigan was another story. For over five hours, I calmed myself by talking to the animals as we crept through whiteouts and buffeting winds. I arrived at the rented house late in the day and plowed with my Toyota into the snowy driveway. A bank of snow and ice blocked the garage door, making it impossible for me to move the car into shelter. It would be six weeks before the car would see the inside of the garage. Although my landlords had made some vague mention that the renters of the upstairs apartment were supposed to keep the drive and walk shoveled, there was no evidence of such an agreement. I waded up steps to the back door and to my new home. The house wasn't exactly like the bungalow in the picture, but it had shingles and sat on a hill overlooking the Crooked River. I had to wait awhile for summer, but when it finally arrived, I planted nasturtiums down by the driveway and put pots of geraniums on the front porch.

I was no longer a recently divorced woman, clearing out the remnants of a nineteen-year marriage. I was a woman in her forty-ninth year facing the future with optimism and a sense of peace.

# PICKING UP THE TRAIL

## *Mauston, Wisconsin May 19–21, 1997*

On May 19, I set off in my Toyota to drive through a gray, glum northern Michigan morning, across the Upper Peninsula with my headlights on. The rain made me sleepy; I longed to pull off the road and take a nap. But I had miles to go—about 425. Driving across the U.P. was new to me, less frightening than I'd expected. I stopped for lunch in Menominee at a sub sandwich shop attached to a brand new Amoco gas station. The bathroom was immaculate—a bowl of potpourri on the sink counter. While I waited for my chicken club sub, the woman behind the counter brought around some homemade cinnamon rolls. It wasn't the run-of-the-mill fast-food joint.

I was headed for Mauston and the Lemonweir Valley. This was the point of departure of the Cole wagons and I wanted to do some preliminary research before setting out on the big journey. My mother had talked about visiting relatives in Mauston when she was a child in the twenties and thir-ties. If I could locate the original family farm site and find out which way they had left the area, I would consider this mission a success. As I drove into Wisconsin, the search took on a different texture. The landscape was gentler than northern Michigan, the trees a bit greener. It was unseasonably cool. I hoped their leaving on April 27, 1871, was fairer. After eight-and-a-half hours on the road, I pulled into Mauston. I felt immediately connected and knew I'd get everything I needed. That protection, grace, call it what you will, was with me during my days there.

I stopped at the public library to inquire about a local historical society. The genealogy group had just left, I was told. I was given the number of Nancy McCullick, who in turn directed me to Merton Eberlein.

I checked in at the Alaskan Motor Inn and called Mr. Eberlein. I could tell he was elderly as we spoke on the phone. I found his white, green-shuttered house easily enough. The Lemonweir River ran behind it. His house was filled with scrapbooks and notebooks of Mauston's history. The information was confusing. Too many Levis and Georges. I kept getting the generations mixed up. The Levi Cole farm was the southwest corner of section 10, now on the north side of State Road 82. This must have been the Levi who was the son of the original Father Cole that Sarah mentioned. Levi Jr. would have been given forty acres. The place was marked by Lone Rock. Mr. Eberlein believed the wagons would have taken the "Sand Road to Lisbon," now called County Road B. Then they would have taken County Road A … on to La Crosse, where a ferry took wagons across the river.

Merton Eberlein had been a postal inspector in South Dakota and Minnesota, then in Wisconsin. He had also been a mail dispatcher on trains. He was ninety-four and had Parkinson's disease but commanded an enormous memory for names and dates, even though they sometimes overlapped and jammed up in the telling. He was a contemporary of Levi Jr.'s grandsons, Ernie and Arthur. He was present during one of their pranks. Grandfather Cole kept a muzzle-loading shotgun locked up; he used it for shooting sparrows. The grandsons got the padlock loose and filled the muzzle with shingle nails. When the grandfather next aimed at sparrows, he peppered the side of the barn with nails. Mr. Eberlein could barely get the story out for laughing.

He also remembered the cyclone of 1913 that tipped all the barns into the river. One square-built barn was more easily righted by the townsmen than were the other structures.

Merton Eberlein pulled himself up with his walker and we stepped out onto the porch. He pointed to the houses on Winsor Street where Levi Jr. and his son George lived: the white one with wooden spoolwork on the porch and on its right the yellow house where the son lived. This Levi was the Cole who stayed behind. His son George was the nephew of George Washington Cole, who left for Minnesota.

I skimmed a profile of Levi R. Cole that Mr. Eberlein had set aside. His farm had been at Lone Rock in the town of Lindina, southwest of Mauston, formerly called Maughs Mills. He died in 1927 at the age of eighty-eight. He was born in 1839 in West Troy, New York. George W. Cole of Pelican Rapids was the younger brother of Levi. Mr. Eberlein believed the third brother was killed in 1862 by the Sioux in the New Ulm Massacre. He said this brother never married.

Mr. Eberlein's account of the other brother didn't fit with what Sarah wrote about the "eldest" brother, along with his wife and children, making the trip to Minnesota. All three sons of Levi Sr. were accounted for in 1871, so who was killed in the massacre in 1862? The obituary implied that Levi was the oldest of the three sons, but as I'd come to know, obits weren't always the most accurate sources. All my family documents put Levi as the middle son. This Cole was a friend of Chief Decorah. He had three children: George H. Cole, at whose home he died; Dr. Alvin V. Cole of Chicago; and Mrs. R.E. Goodhouse; as well as three grandchildren.

Today Mauston, known as Maugh's Mills until 1856 when the U.S. Post Office officially recognized the name change, has a population of 3,439. Captain Milton M. Maughs (1800–1863), a veteran of the Indian Wars, was known as "General" Maughs in the vicinity. Although not the first settler in the area, he gets credit as being the town's founder. He had been part of the Illinois militia during the Black Hawk War. In 1849 he took over the mill on the Lemonweir River that had been operated by Joseph Hewlett, who died that same year. In 1850, the year that Levi and Hannah Cole moved from Walworth County to Juneau County, Maughs moved his family into a "slab shanty on River Street."[8] The name Mauston was created by the "General," dropping the *gh* in his name and adding *-ton*.

The town nestles in the Lemonweir Valley, through which runs the Lemonweir River whose name has its origins with the French fur traders and with Winnebago and Menominee, who held title to the land. *Lemonweir* is probably a corruption of an Indian phrase or a French one, or a combination. In any case, the name has nothing to do with lemons.

That evening after watching a rerun of *Law & Order* in my motel room, I was ready to be alone with all this new information. Mr. Eberlein said that state roads were established back then. They may not have been named, but some kind of trail existed. The state roads were later taken over by the counties. Meeting Merton Eberlein was to touch my ancestors. They became flesh and blood. His stories had more of an effect on me than my mother's or aunts' stories, perhaps because someone outside the family was needed for validity; perhaps because his recollections were not wrapped in a mist of sadness and nostalgia that seemed to accompany the family tales to which I was privy. His house, like houses of old people, was silent, except for a clock ticking in another room. Even the river behind the house was silent, although as I stood up and looked across the sloping yard, I saw a boy scoop up a yellow puppy as it emerged from the water. The upholstered furniture and carpets and drapes sucked up all sound that may have been created down by the riverbank. And it was too chilly for open windows. The air had the too warm, dry atmosphere of elderly people whose lives have become indoor existences.

The next morning I sat at my desk in my room at the Alaskan Motor Inn, listening to traffic on State Road 82 and the voices of women cleaning rooms. Finally the chatter and cigarette smoke outside my door drove me to pack up. Mauston has a surplus of service industry employees—or it may just seem that way because people are friendly and genuinely helpful. At the motel, I saw five women in blue smocks cleaning, and the drugstore had a platoon of employees. Beyond the traffic, I was listening for birds calling, grasses swishing, and wagon wheels creaking under the loads of three households setting out on the Sand Road to Lisbon. I was seeing the orchards full of buds and hearing the weeping of those who stayed behind, who had not been infected with "Minnesota fever" and who watched their loved ones set off west.

My mother and I had a date in Mauston. She was stopping for the night on the way to Ontario, Canada, to visit her eldest sister, who lived in a nursing home. It was this sister who had given me my first copy of Sarah's writings. I'd asked Mr. Eberlein if I could visit him again and bring along my mother, a Cole, a granddaughter of Sarah and George. He was more than willing. My hopes were that this short meeting between me and my mother would celebrate a period of peace. Our relationship had always been knotty. However, since my fiftieth birthday, we'd achieved an equilibrium. Our squabbles were less frequent and less bitter. I'd learned to not unleash my political and religious views. She'd become less prone to provoking me to unleash these opinions. This Mauston visit would be free of opinion and conviction. We'd be here to learn about our ancestors. What they did or did not do could not hurt us the way my mother and I could hurt each other. I suggested this meeting to Mom, half expecting she wouldn't want to take the extra time on her long drive to Ontario. In the past, I've often decided against doing things with her in order to avoid confrontations and disagreements. Now I didn't see how I could really move ahead in exploring the Coles, who were after all her ancestors before they were mine, without including her in the project.

I checked into a roomier place for me and Mom at the Country Inn. It had a small pool, so I could get some exercise for my temperamental back. I also decided to locate Lone Rock, the marker for the Cole farm. I received a variety of directions. The name is popular around Mauston. I decided to trust Merton's directions over those of the Castle Rock Realty people, who told me that Lone Rock is off of U.S. Highway 12 near Sixth Avenue, where there is now a Lone Rock Baptist Church. Going out on State Road 82W, I saw little red signs proclaiming "Town of Lindina" with a W and a four-digit number in the yards of houses. (These numbers were used by the fire department for quick identification.) Brux Orchards caught my eye, mainly because of the huge rock, like the section of a mountain, rising behind the old barn. The woman running it was a Brux (pronounced Brooks). Her mother's father, Elmer Niles, was married in 1899 and purchased the farm shortly afterward. I learned later from Merton that Niles bought it from Levi Cole. It made me happy to think the current orchard could be descended from the apple trees brought from New York by Levi Cole Sr. At one time, orchards and a school bore the name of Lone Rock.

Lunch was at the Roman Castle, where nothing was Roman nor castle-like, just across the road from the Alaskan Motor Inn. I slid into a booth behind two Wisconsin state troopers. The buzz of lunchtime conversations wiped out the contemplative mood of being on Cole land out at Lone Rock. I couldn't help but eavesdrop on the female state trooper's monologue to her tall, fair Dudley Do-Right companion, who murmured assents now and then. She obviously had seniority and was dispensing her experiences between bites on her cheeseburger. I was relieved when they finally put on their hats and left.

I had a list of questions to ask Mr. Eberlein, who referred to himself as a historiographer, during the afternoon visit. Inconsistencies and little mysteries kept cropping up. I was rather protective of these mysteries, reluctant to spend energy dotting the i's and crossing the t's. Why should my relatives be any less mysterious than major historical figures? It seemed disrespectful to probe and dig until I got their lives into an orderly sequence. I wanted some

21

messiness. I never could know it all, because I wasn't there. The *facts* depend on who is doing the recording or telling. Most of my information was from Sarah, who wrote it down decades after arriving in Pelican Rapids.

Merton Eberlein's recollections during our meeting the day before had gelled into vivid, midwestern gothic images: Levi Cole Jr. (the grandfather of his childhood chums) floating in the Lemonweir with his long white beard resting on the water; Levi sleeping with potatoes to keep them from freezing; and George Henry, Levi's son, breaking his ankle while skating on the river and being forever crippled, while the girl with him drowns. According to Mr. Eberlein, Levi did not live on his forty acres after his marriage in 1865 to Frances Risdon. At that point, he went to Werner to work in the sawmill for three or four years, apparently returning to Lone Rock after that.

When my mother and I knocked on the door, the house was as quiet as the previous day. Because he had difficulty getting out of his chair and his part-time housekeeper wasn't there, we let ourselves in. Mom and I sat in the still, airless living room, full of easy chairs and framed photographs. A sunporch, filled with shelves, file cabinets, and teetering stacks of albums and scrapbooks, was Mr. Eberlein's office. Wooden shelves sagged under the weight of heavy notebooks, alphabetized according to family names. The file cabinets were crammed; the couch held papers and folders of tax records, marriage licenses, census reports. Mr. Eberlein instructed me from the living room: "Go to the stack of scrapbooks to the left of the couch. The third one up from the floor. I think it's brown." I fetched the folder, and he carefully turned the yellowed pages with the obituaries clinging to them, like spiderwebs to the side of a house. He passed the scrapbook to me, and I received it like a sacrament, reading about Levi Cole, the brother of my great-grand-father. These two Cole brothers died within three days of each other, one in Wisconsin and one in Minnesota. A section of Levi's obituary from the Mauston newspaper in 1927 gave a glimpse of the Cole brother who stayed behind:

*Levi Cole retired from farming and moved to this city over thirty years ago. He selected as a site for his home a lot on Winsor street which sloped gradually to the channel of the river, one of the finest home sites in Mauston. He loved Nature in all her moods and took great pleasure in watching the development of all natural*

22

*things: The trees, the flowers, buds and fruits and various things of which few have little knowledge were open books to him and he had a broad knowledge of botany and was a keen observer of everything that occurred. He was an interesting talker and it was a pleasure to sit and listen to him recount incidents of the early days during settlement of this community and he remembered clearly many which occurred during the pilgrimage here from New York State. He remembered well and could paint a vivid word picture of the first few days he spent on the farm while his father went back to Walworth county for the rest of the family and how the Indians used to come down over the bluffs thru the woods and scare him and the oxen. They were friendly and it was a great joke to them and he got as much fun out of telling it in later years as they did then. The late Chief Decorah was a friend of his young manhood as he was of many of the young men of that day. He was a kindly, gentle, well intentioned man who lived his life with the desire to be alright and honest and at peace with his fellow.*

I passed the scrapbook to Mom as I looked over another. We kept asking him to repeat things when his sentences jammed up. He was patient. "That's right" and "Oh, no, that wouldn't have been the case." He didn't mind if I turned on my tape recorder. In between conversation, the only sound was the ticking clock, muffled by upholstery and carpets, and the brushing of fingers on old pages.

The next day Mom headed north to Canada. I had taken a photo of her in the orchard with Lone Rock rising behind. Merton Eberlein gave me the name of Levi Jr.'s great-granddaughter who lived in nearby Tomah. I wondered if Levi ever went out and visited his transplanted relatives in Minnesota? What kind of contact was maintained? I called Cynthe Sundin, who was sixty-two and now a grandmother. From our conversation, I got the feeling that I wouldn't learn a lot about the emigrants; her knowledge centered around the Mauston Coles. Her passion was breeding, buying, and showing dogs. We promised to meet next time I was in Mauston.

I called Mr. Eberlein from a pay phone in the Juneau County Courthouse on my way out of town. I was feeling guilty for giving the Leonards short shrift. No, he didn't know of any Leonards who had had a farm by Lone Rock. Nor had he heard of a Mel Leonard, Sarah's brother. I spent an hour in the Mauston Public Library reading through Cole family letters that I had brought with me. Most were to or from Georgina Cole, a prolific letter writer. I liked to think that part of my writing gene came from her. One letter I set aside, in which she mentioned visiting the place at Lone Rock where she was born. She said some complimentary things about Arthur Cole (a true Cole, according to her) and some not so complimentary things about his brother, Ernest, Cynthe's father, whom she thought was more of a Risdon.

Mom and I enjoyed our less-than-twenty-four-hour get-together. She was rather vague on details of family connections, blaming it on being the youngest. She's ten years younger than her sister Beth, eight years younger than Ruth. She never met Sarah, who died before she was born, and she didn't remember meeting her grandfather. She remembered visiting cousins here—whether they were Coles, Leonards, or perhaps DePochees was unclear. The houses on Winsor Street looked vaguely familiar, but she also remembered visiting relatives who had a place on a lake. Perhaps her sisters would remember names more clearly. Before I checked out of the Country Inn, I made a list of all the Leonards in the phone book.

I jotted down the tentative trail to follow next time I came to Mauston—the following year was my plan. I wanted to leave on the same day, April 27, as the three wagons, but doubted if my teaching schedule would allow that early of a departure.

Tentative directions for getting from Mauston to Pelican Rapids:

1. State Road 82W out of Mauston to Lone Rock.
2. Right on Felland Road, behind Lone Rock at Brux Orchards.
3. Take Sand Road to New Lisbon (or just plain Lisbon?).
4. Take County Road B.
5. Take County Road A, through Tomah and Sparta, all the way to La Crosse, the bridge across Mississippi.
6. Take U.S. Highway 61 to St. Paul, following river.
7. Pick up I-94 to Fergus Falls.
8. Take another road on to Pelican Rapids.

According to Mr. Eberlein, the wagons crossed Minnesota on a trail that is now Interstate 94. I felt some urgency to make the trip soon. I was nervous that the opportunity would be snatched away; a year seemed too far off.

I drove from Mauston to Escanaba in the U.P. and checked in at the Hiawatha Motel (nice firm bed) where I called Norm and told him I'd be home tomorrow. We'd just become engaged, having met the previous October in northern Michigan. We had both moved to Emmet County from Pennsylvania. In fact, for over twenty years, we lived five miles apart but were unaware of the other's existence. I felt I was moving back in time to follow Sarah—and journeying into the future in a second marriage with Norm.

# BIG CITY LIGHTS

### Lone Rock to St. Paul: Two Weeks
### April, May 1871

*Now that journey to me was a picnic. I enjoyed every bit of it to the utmost, couldn't help it. We reached St. Paul one Saturday afternoon, after about two weeks travel and camping out, and camped there over Sunday. I chafed in mind because I could not see the city more than just passing through.*

—Sarah Moore Leonard Cole

St. Paul was first known as Pig's Eye, the nickname of trader Pierre Parrant, the first settler. In 1841, Father Lucien Galtier gave it a saint's name when he built the first church. The distance from Lone Rock to St. Paul is about 213 miles. With rough calculations, that works out to about fifteen miles a day by wagon. When the Coles reached the Mississippi River at La Crosse, the wagons were ferried across to the Minnesota side. (By 1876 there was a railroad bridge, but a bridge for wagons wasn't constructed until 1891.) Once in Minnesota, the wagons followed the river. The huge river and overlooking bluffs were an intimidating sight after the serenity of the Lemonweir and the familiar contours of Juneau County.

The Coles left Wisconsin when the railroad was a necessary part of county commerce, and Juneau County's population was well over twelve thousand 12,000. Between 1856 and 1857, the La Crosse and Milwaukee Railroad, known as the Milwaukee Road, was built. Many farmers were persuaded to mortgage their farms and buy stock in the new company. After all, they would be beneficiaries of the new mode of transportation. However, after over a million dollars of farm money was invested, the railroad declared bankruptcy and foreclosures followed. By 1859, the Milwaukee Road had

come through its financial crisis and regular passenger and freight service
ran through Mauston and New Lisbon. Train whistles played counterpoint
to the creak of wagon wheels on that spring day in 1871. In that year, the
railroad company bought fifty thousand railroad ties at 35 each from Juneau
County woodcutters.[9]

From Sarah's report, it seems they camped outside the city, perhaps at Fort
Snelling. The city had grown around the fort, established in 1819 to pro-
tect the headquarters of the American Fur Company. The fort commanded
a view of the confluence of the Minnesota and Mississippi Rivers. Zebu-
lon Pike recognized its military importance back in 1805 when he selected
the site, which was considered the gateway to the Northwest. The city was
prosperous when the Coles passed through in 1871, mainly due to the economic driving force of railroad builder James J. Hill. The St. Paul and Pacific
Railroad began its first ten-mile run in 1862. It's possible that their wagons crossed these railroad tracks on the journey west. St. Paul had been the
capital city since 1858, when Minnesota was given statehood, and by 1870,
thanks to the coming of the railroad, it was a developed distribution center
with some of the largest wholesale and jobbing houses in the country.[10] This
was probably the largest city the Coles had seen. Its 1870 population was
20,030, compared to Minneapolis's 13,066.[11] And by this time government
dams and locks had been constructed, so they must have witnessed a water-
way with traffic, not a wild, deserted river.

If they did stay outside the city at Fort Snelling, was it for safety reasons?
Was the threat of Indian attack a concern in 1871? Probably not. By then
most of the tribes of Wisconsin and Minnesota had been bought out, relocated, or wiped out. The Fort Snelling of 1871 was not the active outpost of
previous decades when combat between whites and natives was a common
occurrence. In fact, by the 1870s, the headquarters and officers were located
in St. Paul, with noncommissioned personnel working out of the fort. However, the Sioux Uprising, of which the New Ulm Massacre gained the most
notoriety, had occurred less than ten years before. There had been past treaties between the U.S. government and the Sioux—in 1815, 1825, and 1851.
The Sioux Uprising of 1862 was the culmination of building resentment
toward the ever-growing presence of whites on Sioux land, the corrupt influ-
ences of white culture, and deception by the U.S. government. Numbers

range from five hundred to eight hundred settlers and soldiers killed during a forty-day war; the number of Sioux killed is less clear.

In an account by Charlotte O. Van Cleve, who had grown up near Fort Snelling, she tells of speaking to "Old Shakopee," a Sioux warrior who was lying "with gyves [shackles] upon his legs, in our guard house at Fort Snelling, awaiting execution, for almost numberless cold-blooded murders, perpetrated during the dreadful massacre of '62." This was the concluding event in a longer account of a girlhood experience witnessing the death of another Sioux, "Little Six," who was the father of Old Shakopee.

Little Six was one of a group of Sioux brought to Fort Snelling around 1827 to "stand trial" for the murder of five Chippewa (Ojibwa), killed when their wigwam was fired into, just after the two tribes had smoked the peace pipe together. The punishment was administered by the injured tribe by making the condemned Sioux run for their lives, as Mrs. Van Cleve's eyewitness account tells:

> [W]e stand on tiptoe, while the balls and chains are knocked off and the captives are set free. At one word one of the doomed men starts, the rifles with unerring aim are fired, and under cover of the smoke a man falls dead. They reload, the word is given, another starts with a bound for home; but ah! the aim of those clear-sighted, blood-thirsty red men is too deadly; and so one after another until four are down.
>
> And then the last, 'Little Six'—whom at that distance, we children readily recognize, from his commanding height and graceful form; he is our friend, and we hope he will get home. He starts,—they fire,—the smoke clears away and still he is running,—we clap our hands, and say 'he will get home'; but another volley and our favorite, almost at the goal, springs into the air and comes down—dead![12]

Sarah makes no reference to Indians until they reach western Minnesota. Their migration occurred between the two historic events for the Sioux: the New Ulm Massacre (1862) and the Battle of the Little Bighorn (1876). During their journey in 1871, and even during their homesteading in western Minnesota, the Coles had little to fear from Indians. The references to Native Americans in Sarah's account and in newspaper articles give images of slightly scary encounters or good-natured "friendly" anecdotes. "By 1871 most of the tribes in the United States had signed treaties ceding most or all of their ancestral land in exchange for reservations and welfare,"[13] so these Coles moved through land that had once been home to Winnebago, Menominee, Sioux, Ojibwa. Their journey was one more small step toward separating the Indians from their life and breath: the land.

During their two days of camping in St. Paul, they had hordes of Red River traders for neighbors. In the spring and early fall, the carts, sometimes in caravans of more than a hundred, streamed from the north toward St. Paul, one of the largest fur markets in America. Workers from the Hudson Bay Company all congregated in St. Paul at this time of year.[14] Much of the trading was done outside the city because of mutual distrust between the townspeople and traders. Larpenteur's Lake was a popular campsite.[15] But Sarah was impressed by the city and wanted to linger a while before embarking on the most strenuous part of the trip.

## *Lone Rock to St. Paul: Seven-and-a-half Hours (Including a stop in Tomah) June 1998*

**June 15, 16**

After a night and a morning of packing, Norm and I left our home in the northern part of Michigan's Lower Peninsula. Again, as when I left Pennsylvania for Michigan in 1996, I mentally compared the Camry's contents with Sarah's inventory of the prairie schooner:

| Marla and Norm | Sarah |
|---|---|
| Laptop | Bureau packed with dry goods |
| Minolta camera | 35 yards new rag carpeting |
| Tape recorder | Barrel full of dishes |
| Picnic basket | Keg of soft soap |
| Coffee maker | Bushel of "early rose" seed potatoes |
| Beach chairs | High chair |
| Two suitcases of clothes | Rocking chair |
| Pillows | Husband's chair |

Small cooler                Team of horses
Hiking boots                Two cows
Travel iron                 French pony
Wine and corkscrew          Hens and ducks
Granola bars
Sunscreen, insect repellent
Bathing suits
Books
Notebook paper
AAA maps and TripTiks
Box of research (old family letters,
    Sarah's account)

Although Sarah's list was shorter, it named all her worldly goods. My list was only a portion of my possessions. They were things for a brief expedition away from home. I had an address where I would return—a house with dishes in the cupboard and books on the shelves. Sarah had given up all settled comforts.

We crossed the Mighty Mac over the Straits, driving across the U.P. to Menominee where we stayed overnight with Norm's brother and wife. At first I resisted this stop. I wanted to get right into "the Project," driving straight to Lone Rock and leaving from there. But I had to remind myself that Sarah traveled with her in-laws; the whole move was a family enterprise. So, I forced myself to slow down and enjoy the trip. I didn't want to be so documentary-obsessed that I lost sight of the beauty of the land and the *feel* of migrating. Jim and Sharon took us out to dinner and gave us a tour of Menominee, with anecdotes about the town's living and dead citizens.

We reached Mauston by the same route I had taken thirteen months before. I felt as if I were going home. I wasn't traveling with that heightened awareness and speeded-up energy level I experienced when I was on the road alone. I was glad to have my husband of six months with me, a steady companion and eager helper.

The territory between Menominee and Mauston was not wholly unfamiliar to Norm either. His first wife had grown up in Wisconsin, and as we drove through small towns, the names struck a chord with him. We drove past an old hotel, dilapidated and forgotten, where his former father-in-law had stayed on insurance-selling trips. In some ways we were bringing our former spouses along on the journey, the memories of other trips trailing along behind us.

We drove through Ripon and past the little white schoolhouse, which bore the distinction of the "birthplace of the Republican Party." Somewhere after Ripon, we stopped at the only restaurant in a small town. "Raspberry pie," I said, pointing excitedly at the menu. The restaurant was full. All the municipal workers in their green uniforms sat around a large table near our booth. We were discreetly noticed as strangers. We could feel it in the slight lifting of gazes, then we were ignored. The pie was advertised as homemade. Norm and I each ordered a piece after our sandwiches. "It's real good," the waitress had assured us. It was awful—garish red Jell-O filling on a tough, unyielding crust. So as not to offend our enthusiastic waitress, we both cleaned our plates.

We arrived in Mauston around 1:30, settled on the cheapest of the inns, the Alaskan Motor Lodge, Motel, Restaurant, Bowling Alley, etc., where I'd stayed the previous year. Only $44/night. After checking in, we set out on a dress rehearsal for the morning's prairie schooner departure.

We went as far as Hustler. We drove out State Road 82W to Felland Road, on the backside of Lone Rock, then took pretty Felland to Sand Road, which goes to New Lisbon, except you don't get all the way to New Lisbon on this road. Then County Road B to County Road A, which leads to Hustler. There at the store/post office, a friendly man behind the counter told me how to take a detour to Tomah so I could meet Cynthe Sundin, a Cole relative. It wouldn't be truly authentic, but after Tomah, we could get back to the "original" route.

During my 1997 trip to Mauston, I'd taken a couple of back roads from Lone Rock, but had not ventured this far. Perhaps I was over-preparing, but I wanted to head out the way the wagons had. At the same time, I didn't want to lay out the trip too perfectly. I wanted to maintain a sense of adventure. I couldn't duplicate the wagon trail perfectly, but I could follow the clues I had and do my best.

From Sarah's account and from obituaries Mr. Eberlein had shared, I thought I knew who were in the three wagons which headed out on April

27: the elders, Levi and Hannah Catherine Van Arnam Cole; their oldest son, William Henry, and wife, Mary E. Cady, and their children (they had eight but all were not born by 1871); and George Washington Cole and wife, Sarah Leonard, and their baby girl, Georgina.

Before dinner we drove over to the Mauston Cemetery on Martin Street. Our shoes grew damp and our souls peaceful wandering through the old section. With birds flitting from tree to tree and the sky moving into soft twilight pinks and lavenders, we found some Coles: Emma L. Cole (April 2, 1866–Jan. 19, 1888); Elias Cole, marked by a big pink tippy stone monument (died Dec. 19, 1895, at 86 yrs. 9 mos. 20 days); Eddy Cole, a Civil War vet with a GAR marker (died Dec. 6, 1880, at 45 years). I was grateful for the nineteenth-century method of documenting the deceased's span of life on the stone. More and more I relied on cemeteries to piece together the scraps of family mythology. Elias Cole was the brother of Levi Sr. Eddy must have been Elias's son, named after Elias's father, who had kept the post office in Hoffman's Ferry, New York, and had taken his son Levi to see General Lafayette. And Emma who died at twenty-one? Had she been the second Eddy's daughter?

We also came upon the founder of Mauston, Capt. Milton Maughs, who began the town on April 25, 1856. Milton M. Maughs: Capt. 27 Regt. Ill. Inf. Indian Wars. Oct. 2, 1800–Feb. 18, 1863. Reading the weathered stones in the soft, waning light extended the calm, low-key mood of the trip so far. I had left my novels at home, even my tapes. The car radio had been silent. I'd found my desire for constant stimulation and distractions diminishing. I was resisting all urges to speed up travel. Progress and technology had changed the landscape forever. The only thing I could control was my mind. By shutting out as many distractions as possible, I hoped to be more open to the mood of the wagon trip, better able to focus on Sarah and more receptive to what she was still able to communicate to a great-granddaughter.

We ate dinner at the Alaskan Restaurant and learned the reason for the name. The owners' son told us his parents had lived in Alaska when they were young. The love of Alaska was evident in the decor—a lodge-like ambience with photos, bright landscape paintings, and Indian carvings. I thought it rather sad—having such strong yearnings for a place other than where you live. The son had never been to Alaska. In a way, Michigan was my Alaska; I fantasized for years of moving back, and I finally had. Minnesota was Sarah's Alaska. We had both left a settled life to go to a place we yearned to be.

# June 17

After breakfast at the Roman Castle, where I'd lunched over a year before, we headed out to Lone Rock for our official departure. We took pictures of Brux Orchards, trying to imagine how the Cole land had looked in 1871. (We lost that roll of film somewhere along the trail.) It felt anticlimactic. Shouldn't there be a fanfare, some sending off? I tooted my Toyota's horn a couple of times and reset the trip meter as we turned down the smooth pavement of Felland Road. We took the country roads, passing hardly any other cars. After Hustler, we crossed the winding Lemonweir River. It took us 24.4 miles to reach State Route 131, our detour to Tomah.

Driving through Wisconsin on county roads on a June morning can restore a person's image of America as a farming nation. Barns, silos, corn cribs, tractors, harvesters, plows, manure, cows. Wisconsin's roads, even the narrow back roads, were well-maintained, no potholes. Mr. Eberlein had told me that there was a system of roads in the 1870s, so the Coles were not rolling over rutted fissures in the earth as they headed for the Mississippi. Still my trip had more security; I know there are roads that will get me to Pelican Rapids. The Coles didn't even know that they'd end up there.

Even with the tame conditions of my 1998 trip, I felt the high of risk-taking. Surely, Sarah felt this as she peered out from the canvas of the prairie schooner. I was being risky in just following my wishes. It felt good to view life as an adventure. I remembered how exhilarated I'd felt after college graduation when I traveled to West Africa to teach with the Peace Corps. Kind of like jumping off a cliff. Somewhere along the way, as I moved toward middle age, I had lost the will to take risks, those risks that sprang from inner stirrings. I couldn't have followed my great-grandmother five years before. It would have been a crazy idea, too "selfish." For much of my adult life, I had done the most practical, the most sensible thing. I had been dutiful to my own detriment. I had needed an "unsettling" to shake me up. It had taken me a long time, with many painful lessons, to learn this big one: listening to your gut desires, your yearnings, will lead you to the best decisions.

On the way to Tomah on State Route 131, we passed the Council Creek Emu Farm and glimpsed the huge birds moving behind a fence, like prisoners in a foreign country. Tomah was a neat, orderly town. We followed Cynthe's directions, between the high school and hospital, to her house near Lake Tomah, where the Lemonweir River makes another appearance as it joins with the lake. Cynthe Sundin, great-granddaughter of Levi Jr., ushered us into her dining room. Her house had a museum-like quality, filled with antiques. Even the bathroom was stocked with curios, offering an alternative to magazine reading. As she served us coffee and Danishes, I sensed we were checking out each other for signs of "Coleness," whatever that was—perhaps a lift of the eyebrow, an inflection in the voice, a set of the jaw. I remembered the letter from Georgina in which she fastened the label "a true Cole" to Cynthe's uncle. I wondered what her criteria were.

Cynthe had sent me a packet last year after our telephone conversation. It contained a family tree, some obituaries, and other newspaper clippings. Some of the information had been provided by Georgina Cole Harris, Sarah and George's "baby in the wagon." Georgina turned out to be a family historian, dispersing information about the Coles all the way back to James Cole, who came from England in 1633 to settle in Plymouth, Massachusetts. As we sat at Cynthe's table, we talked only of the present. From her dining room window we could see her two yellow Labradors and black lab puppy enjoying the sunshine outside their own houses in the backyard. Her conversation was sprinkled with "bitches," "majors" at dog shows, doing "confirmations," "good trainers." Her husband had died the previous September, so she was keeping busy. She lent me a book on Juneau County's centennial, edited by Merton Eberlein, who was a friend of her parents. I didn't feel any real family connection, but I felt we had made a human, friendly encounter. Norm took our picture together in front of her van.

"Let's pick up 16 here in Tomah. It will be easier to get to La Crosse," said Norm as we fastened our seat belts. But I was stubborn. "The Coles wouldn't have come through Tomah. We need to go back to County A, and then pick up 16." I could tell he didn't agree with my insistence on authenticity, but I was behind the wheel. I stopped on County Road A to take a picture of a radio tower, simply because it was so out of keeping with Wisconsin's 1871 landscape. My stubbornness was wasted and authenticity went to hell when after getting onto State Highway 16W, detour signs directed us to State Highway 21, a road which went past Fort McCoy.

Since we'd been forced off the trail, we decided to make the most of it. We passed a field of giant animals in the unincorporated town of Angelo. We were intrigued enough to turn around and pull into the parking lot of the F.A.S.T. Corp. Although there were several acres filled with mammoth fiberglass animals and figures, the company seemed to be producing more. A few workers moved around a large, garage-like building. The "sculptures"— giant cowboy boots, giraffes, chickens, horses, two tomatoes—were in various states of health. Some were toppled, some faded and weather-beaten. A huge sign told visitors they could wander around and photograph things— but at their own risk. It was compellingly surreal. Norm took a picture of me touching my finger to the oversize finger of a fiberglass E.T. (This picture was also on the lost roll.)

We headed off again through rich farmland, past Amish buggies and wagons, and huge farms, rolling countryside. Now I could hear clearly the wagons of 1871 because twentieth-century technology had been kept at bay. The earth and air proclaimed fertility and abundance.

We had come 89.4 miles when we reached downtown La Crosse. We had lunch at a restaurant where the tables gave off a whiff of chlorine from the waiter's rag and the dubious Cobb salad was based on pale iceberg lettuce. According to our TripTik, it was 345.9 miles from La Crosse to Pelican Rapids, the travel time six hours and forty-five minutes. I thought of the three Cole wagons facing another five-and-a-half weeks of travel. Here at La Crosse their wagons had been ferried across.

Even though our trip by bridge over the Mississippi was too quick for contemplation, I marveled at the huge river, a country in itself, moving beneath us. I regretted that we couldn't cross by ferry. Being high over the water removed us from the experience of crossing, of moving over the surface of the river. We pulled into a park on the Minnesota side. A man tossed a miniature football to his little boy, a woman walked her obese dog, a teen rubbed sunscreen on the freckled back of his girlfriend, motorboats buzzed out on the water, cars whizzed by on U.S. 61. Our leisurely trip had ended.

Sarah and George must have been in awe of the scenery. How had the face of the Mississippi changed? Undoubtedly the high bluffs and outcroppings were there, but were there islands, little formations in the river? The sound of the Mississippi moving beneath them must have been validation that they had really left their Wisconsin home behind. We stopped at Lock and Dam Number 5, built by the U.S. Army Corps of Engineers long after the Coles passed by.

I resisted the impulse to stop at every historical site and museum on the way up U.S. 61.

Was the trail along U.S. 61N, or was it down closer to the water where the railroad runs? The trip already seemed long to us, and we'd been gone only two days.

As we became a part of the rush-hour congestion on I-494, I wondered what Sarah would think of all this stop-and-go traffic? It was hard to imagine open prairie and silence in this spot. Sarah was all for progress and civilization, but I doubt she could have imagined this.

Did Sarah and George experience traveling friction? Did she tell him how to drive the team? I found myself getting anxious with Norm at the wheel of my Camry. I tried hard to keep my mouth shut and succeeded about half the time. "Don't you think you should be in third?" "I don't usually put it in fifth until I get up to forty-five or fifty." Somehow our mutual annoyances never set into bitterness. We were able to travel over the little bumps.

We would be staying for two nights at Mary and Audrey's townhouse in Edina, just outside the Twin Cities. Mary is Norm's former sister-in-law, his first wife's sister. She and Audrey have shared living arrangements since they graduated from college. After Norm's first wife died, he spent time with Mary and Audrey. It is an important bond, and there was no reason why a second marriage should weaken it. Likewise, I have maintained ties with my former sister-in-law, the sister of my first husband. She and I had remained friends through and after my divorce from her brother. Sarah Cole never experienced an extended family quite like mine. The sadness of broken relationships has been softened by forming new ones—when the trails become rough, it's up to us to make them smoother.

## *June 18*

Off the trail in Edina. Audrey chauffeured me into St. Paul to the Minnesota History Center, run by the Minnesota Historical Society. Sarah had wanted to spend more time in the city, but the demands of the journey did not allow it. I would see the city for her. A green sign told me that St. Paul had a population of over 272,000—a bit more than in 1871. (In 1870 the population was 20,030; by 1880 it had more than doubled to 41,473.) I quickly got my feet wet in the waters of research when I read all the rules for using the archives. I put my things in a locker—only notebooks and pencils were allowed into the two rooms of the library. I tried the Ronald M. Hubbs Room first, hoping to read Sarah's original piece as it appeared in the *St. Paul Farmers' Dispatch*. Two and a half hours later, I'd come up with nothing. I had to resist stopping the microfilm reader for stories of murder/suicides on lonely farms; articles about the sinking of the Lusitania and President Wilson's marriage to Mrs. Galt; ads for Piper Heidsieck tobacco ("with a taste of champagne"); and cures for catarrh, piles, deafness, deformity, ruptures, you name it. The biweekly paper, which came out on Tuesdays and Fridays and called itself "An Educational, Agricultural Newspaper," had a circulation of 200,000. It contained serials, such as "Danger" by A. Conan Doyle. There were advice columns for young ladies and dress patterns which could be ordered for 10 cents. There were ads for a Year-Book, which might have contained Sarah's piece. If I was able to return on another day, I could check the *Pioneer Press*. Audrey read this newspaper as a child. *The Farmers' Dispatch* and the *Pioneer Press* were part of the same company. Perhaps Pelican Rapids would have a copy, so I wouldn't have to go blind while reading old newspapers on microfilm.

I could have missed Sarah's piece in the newspaper. I went through every issue, two a week, for 1915. But it was difficult to spot things readily. The reader had to be adjusted constantly to take in the whole page, and the newspapers of 1915 were not organized as tidily as today's. In some ways it was a disappointing day. I expected to find lots on the Coles in the new, impressive History Center. I found a Georgiana Cole of Ramsey County in the biographical file of the Weyerhaeuser Reference Room, but she was born in

1832, and as far as I know, none of my Coles had settled in Ramsey County. I knew I'd need at least a week in St. Paul just to learn how to use the resources.

Mary and Audrey were putting a new room off their dining room. It had a "solar tube" for extra light—better than a skylight. At the end of the day, we sat talking about the construction of the new room and drinking gin and tonics. My mind kept being jerked back to something I came across in the library. It was a grisly counterpoint to my comfortable setting—on a sofa with a drink in hand in a tastefully furnished townhouse. It was in the Weyerhaeuser Room where I was browsing through the *Minnesota Historical Society Collections* (Vol. 3 1870–80) and came across "A Reminiscence of Ft. Snelling" by Mrs. Charlotte O. Van Cleve. The most horrific section was her description of the Chippewa's actions after they had executed five Sioux in a "run for your life" shooting. Up until this point, my sympathies had been with the Chippewa for their dead and wounded, after a sneak attack by the Sioux. Mrs. Van Cleve tells of the images from childhood, around 1827:

> *And now follows a scene that beggars description. The bodies, all warm and limp, are dragged to the row of the hill. Men who at the sight of blood, become almost fiends, tear off the reeking scalps and hand them to the chief, who hangs them around his neck. Women and children with tomahawks and knives cut deep gashes in the poor dead bodies, and scooping up the hot blood with their hands, eagerly drink it; then, grown frantic, they dance, and yell, and sing their horrid scalp songs, recounting deeds of valor on the part of their brave men, and telling off [sic] the Sioux scalps, taken in different battles until tired and satiated at last with their horrid feast, they leave the mutilated bodies—festering in the sun.*
>
> *At nightfall they are thrown over the bluff into the river, and my brother and myself, awe struck and quiet, trace their hideous voyage down the Mississippi to the Gulf of Mexico. We lie awake that night talking of the dreadful sight we have seen, and we try to imagine what the people in New Orleans will think when they see those ghastly upturned faces …*

When we stopped at Fort Snelling the next morning, back on the wagon trail, and gazed down to where the Minnesota River meets the Mississippi, I thought of the mutilated Sioux being carried south, their butchered faces to the sky.

On the misty, foggy morning that we stopped at Fort Snelling, there were few tourists. We learned from a tall, bearded staff member that most likely wagons had not stayed overnight in the 1870s. The tour of the fort was based on life in the 1820s, a half century before the Cole wagons rolled through St. Paul. I wanted to stay in an 1870s mood, so we didn't enter the gates for the tour of the restored fort, in which visitors could watch reenactments of everyday life by carpenters, traders, and blacksmiths. Afterwards these same visitors could then drive a few miles and roam the Mall of America.

We picked up bits of information from plaques and brochures: the fort was made of limestone from nearby bluffs and burnt lime was the mortar; the two towers are original structures; the Dakota, or Sioux, called the meeting of the Minnesota and Mississippi Rivers "M'dota"; European fur traders used the rivers for two centuries before the white settlers; the Minnesota River was first known as the St. Peter's.

At the giftshop/bookstore, I bought two books, one on the Red River Trails and one on Minnesota history in the 1870s. I also bought a bag of sassafras tea. The sibilance of "sassafras" created a mood of pioneers and slow trips. I remembered my aunt drinking sassafras tea. Upon closer inspection of the bag's ingredients, I read: licorice root, wood betony, orange peel, cinnamon, rose hips, artificial sassafras flavor, artificial and natural flavor. So much for my sassafras fantasies.

I reset the trip odometer as we drove away from the fort. We had used the car for sixty-two miles worth of driving during our Edina layover. We were ready for the next leg of the journey: St. Paul to Pelican Rapids. It took the Coles four weeks, so they were going slower than their fifteen-miles-a-day rate during the first two weeks of travel. No four-lane interstates for them; no green signs with big white letters saying 230 miles to Pelican Rapids.

# RED RIVER TRAILS

## *May 1871*

*Later I remember we had some adventures; one of the brother's little girls came very near drowning when we camped by the Pomme de Terre River, and we had hard work to resuscitate her. This was the most serious.*

—Sarah Moore Leonard Cole

**T**his incident, from which the girl recovered, did not involve Indians. In spite of Evander Leonard's warnings to Sarah about dangers of attacking tribes, they moved across Minnesota with nary an encounter. They were traveling in relative comfort in a prairie schooner, not the more primitive oxcarts that moved over the rutted paths that formed the unraveled web of Red River Trails, a series of little roads wandering off from larger, more traveled ones. The Coles would have taken the Metropolitan Trail out of the teeming capital and headed for St. Cloud. This route followed the Mississippi, past towns established earlier: Anoka in 1853 and Elk River, which had been the site of a trading post since 1848. The Metropolitan Trail was not a straight-forward route, though not nearly as convoluted as the Middle Trail, a military road which overlapped it.

Near St. Cloud the three Cole wagons had to cross the Mississippi yet again to hook up with the Middle Trail. St. Cloud had three ferries, and at least one of them operated every year after 1855.[16]

The trade on the trails between 1820 and 1870 laid the basis for the coming of the railroads. By the end of 1872, Minnesotan earth was covered with 1,906 miles of railroad tracks.[17] In 1871, as the Coles pushed west in their prairie schooners, the Great Northern (formerly the St. Paul and Pacific Railroad) reached Breckenridge. The Milwaukee and St. Paul came down to

Winona on the Mississippi. And in Hastings, the first iron railroad bridge in Minnesota was completed. The Northern Pacific, the Southern Minnesota, the Winona and St. Peter—all changed the landscape forever. New tracks sprang up all around the Coles. The symbol of industry and expansion may have appeared in the distance as the wagons negotiated the boggy ruts. The use of the trails ended in 1872 when the Northern Pacific was opened to Moorhead, Minnesota.[18] The Coles may have been some of the last pioneers to actually use the trails and to emigrate by covered wagon.

Once off the ferry and onto the Middle Trail, they aimed for Frazee City. The Middle Trail was composed of several tracks and offshoots. The various tracks evolved during different time periods. How did they know which of the myriad paths to follow? They may have taken the section known as the Stage Road to Sauk Centre and then onto the Old Middle Trail that dipped below the Stage Road. It's not certain at what point they crossed the Pomme de Terre River.

The river flows south from Pomme de Terre Lake, and north of that was Pomme de Terre station on the Stage Road. It was subsequently renamed Fort Pomme de Terre, a more lyrical name than Fort Potato, when it became an active site in the wars against the Dakota. If they were approaching Fergus Falls south of the Stage Road, on the Old Middle Trail, they would have had the opportunity to rest at the relatively solid shores of White Bear Lake. The marshy, squishy route had to be wearing on people, not to mention their horses. The area beyond the lake, going toward the Chippewa and Pomme de Terre Rivers, was a pioneer's nightmare. Wagons often avoided the water-laden, roller-coaster topography by going twenty miles out of the way in order to gain ten miles on the actual trail.[19] And small items were often thrown out of the wagons, often only four by fifteen feet, to lighten the load. The prairie must still hold some of these belongings, cast off in the cause of progress.

It was well into May as they made this section of the trip. Prairie schooners did not so much sail as lumber across the prairie, over tussocks and through the tall grasses of western Minnesota. The most common plants were the grasses, with their own minute flowers as well as the ground-hugging forbs: prairie violets, violet wood sorrel, yellow star-grass and the slightly taller valerian. If Sarah had kept a journal during the crossing, she might have provided more details of the colors on the prairie and about her niece's near-drowning. Too chilly to swim in May, the girl must have fallen in, unable to swim. The incident probably made all the adults extra vigilant about the activities of the children for the remainder of the journey.

Whether they followed the Stage Road the whole way, or took a link onto the Old Middle Trail, they had to get off the "main" route to go through Fergus Falls. As of 1870, none of the Middle Trail's branches went through the middle of Fergus Falls. So close to their original destination, they were now disheartened.

> As we came near our promised land we heard discouraging descriptions of Frazee City, that it was only a 'sand pile' etc., and that all the good land in that vicinity was taken up, so our prospects growing cloudy, and we felt very anxious, almost like wanderers on the face of the earth. We passed through Fergus Falls when the town was just starting. There were a few buildings not completed, and the grass was still green in the streets. Buffalo fish were then running in the river, and such a sight as they were! Sturgeons too, I think some of them were five feet long, and they rolled slowly from side to side in the river as we watched them.

## June 19, 1998

Buzzing out of St. Paul toward St. Cloud on I-94, it was hard to maintain that old-timey feeling. We took the St. Cloud exit and followed the food signs on a congested road. At a Boston Market, we ate one of our first fast-food meals of the trip, then pushed the trays to the side to spread out our map from AAA and the maps of the Red River Trails. I-94 most closely approximated the old route from St. Cloud to Fergus Falls, but there was an array of variations to this route, with links and new connecting paths being made every year. Trying to coordinate points on these two different maps gave us a headache. We could only guess at the Coles' route. Of course, no matter which of the many strands of the Middle Trail we chose, we wouldn't be that far off. We were at the end of the Metropolitan Trail and ready for the Middle Trail. On the AAA map, I-94 did not cross the Pomme de Terre River, and I wanted to make contact with every site mentioned in Sarah's account. There weren't that many details, so it was necessary to pay homage to the few written down. At the same time, I didn't want to become so obsessed with historical detail that I ceased enjoying the journey. I wanted Norm to enjoy the trip, and we both were making an effort to relax and take each new twist in the itinerary with calmness and interest. Our trip could never duplicate theirs. Too much time had passed, too much "progress."

We decided to point the Toyota down the Stage Road (still I-94) until Sauk Centre and then take State Highway 28W to Glenwood, where we'd pick up State Highway 55W, or what looked like the Old Middle Trail. Then we could connect with U.S. Highway 59 which would take us into Fergus Falls.

I felt we were on the right track. I could hear the wagons again. We stopped at Kensington, which wasn't founded until 1890, according to the large sign by the highway. Our chosen way took us past the huge Minnewaska Lake, or White Bear Lake as it was called then. The area was marshy, low country. They must have seen all green and blue with a sprinkling of color from wildflowers. Were the cottonwoods littering the ground with their soft, white droppings?

When we found the Pomme de Terre River, we were elated, as happy as if we were the first to ever see it. The tall reeds formed its sides, no real banks of sand or dirt. I picked a small bouquet of yellow vetch, hoary alyssum, and elegant wheat-like grass. Standing beside the sign that named the river as Norm took my picture, I was grateful we were making this trip by car and not by horse and wagon. I imagined Norm and Marla in a prairie schooner lurching over a maze of Red River Trails; Norm grabbing the map every few minutes, compulsively checking the progress of the journey, surveying the land, double-checking the stopping-off places; Marla stubbornly repeating the directions: *follow the river until you come to a town.* She would want to stop for each wildflower and bird she saw and would remind Norm to not drive the horses hard in low gear, to not go uphill (if there were any) in high gear. She would rather be driving the team. When they sank to the axles in a boggy patch near the Pomme de Terre, they'd have a picnic and open a bottle of wine.

We headed for Fergus Falls on U.S. 59 and as we neared it, we somehow got back onto I-94, exited as soon as possible and got turned around on the other side of the town. We weren't seriously lost, but it was the first time since leaving home that we were confused. When we regained our sense of direction, we drove through Fergus, as my mother's relatives refer to it. There was no longer grass in the streets. We located the Otter Tail Historical Society, which has a library with extensive family information. We planned to come back after exploring Pelican Rapids, about twenty-five miles up the road.

As we drove into Pelican, population 1,886, I had the feeling I'd been here, although my mother didn't remember ever bringing me here as a child. It was the same gauzy, gut-familiar sensation I'd had traveling along the Hudson River in New York State—a visceral connection to places my ancestors have lived.

After checking into the Pelican Motel, the only motel, we had dinner at Auntie Ev's. The town was charming without being pretentious. No arugula and sprouts. We had fried chicken and french fries but declined the soft white rolls. The town's business district was intact, unlike so many small midwestern towns off the beaten track. There was a little of everything here: industry (the turkey plant); recreation (parks and a pool); library.

We drove out of town after dinner and stopped at a historical monument. In the waning light, we read that Harrison Harris was credited with being Pelican Rapids' first settler in 1869. The first school district (No. 10) was organized on Nov. 17, 1871, and the village was platted in 1872. Then I saw a familiar name: Louis DePochee. He was the first settler for Lida Township, outside the village proper. George Cole's sister, Mary, married Louis DePochee.

I called my mother to tell her we'd made it and were staying at the Pelican Motel. "That's the hottest place I've ever stayed," she said, recalling a family reunion in the '60s. She didn't know of any Coles living there now. She told me to visit Aunt Tillie's house, "on the left as you go east out of town." She reminded me that Sarah and George settled near Prairie Lake originally, just a few miles outside Pelican. She remembered her father pointing out their farm as they drove out past Dunn's Resort. They moved into town later in life, to a house near their daughter Tillie. The only relative still in Pelican that she knew of was Tillie's daughter-in-law, Mildred Frazee. The phone book for Otter Tail County was full of Coles, but I had no inclination to call any of them, to ask them if they were related to the 1871 Coles. I was satisfied to have reached my "promised land." I felt at home, confident that I would find out what I needed to know.

# PELICAN RAPIDS,
# THEN AND NOW

## June 6, 1871

*The people there told us perhaps we could find some land at Pelican Rapids, about 25 miles farther on, so we moved on, my husband riding Jockey on ahead to look for the place. When we had gone about that distance from Fergus Falls, he on the pony mounted a small elevation or mound for a good look about, when lo! he discovered he was on top of a dug-out, sodded over, and that was Pelican Rapids. So there we halted, June 6, 1871, our baby's birthday. She was just a year old that day.*

*There were a few settlers near, very nice American people, who gave us a hearty welcome and were glad to show and tell us what they knew of the country, and were anxious that we should stop with them. There was good, heavy timber on the east side of the Pelican River which ran through the place, and prairie on the west side. Land was to be had on either side, and it was a question for some time which would be better for us. I think the women decided in favor of the timber land.*

—Sarah Moore Leonard Cole

My Aunt Beth gives a slightly different version of George Cole's inadvertent discovery of Pelican Rapids, in which he stepped onto a mound and noticed a stovepipe protruding from the earth. He finally realized he was standing on a store, the beginning of the town's business district.

The choice of timberland over prairie was in keeping with the custom of settlers before the railroads worked their way beyond the Big Woods. Before the tracks were laid, prairie existence was isolated and far from goods and services. Newcomers were afraid of the barren expanse, of wind and fire. They assumed the soil was poor. Most, like the Coles, labored to clear forested land, then built from the timber.

To have traveled so far to their promised land, only to find that it was already someone else's, then to have to move on in search of a home, must have been discouraging. A land grab was in full swing at the time of their emigration. St. Cloud and Alexandria were Minnesota's busiest land offices between 1865 and 1871.[20] Settlers started returning to the territory after the Civil War ended. The New Ulm Massacre in 1862 had scared off many from their claims, but now it appeared the Indians were less of a threat.

Once they crossed off Frazee City, called just plain "Frazee," from the list, the Coles were ready to stop at the first semi-settled community. Apparently Fergus Falls real estate had all been claimed by the time they arrived, and so they pushed on to a place they had never expected to call home, a place with more pelicans than settlers. More than one lake in Otter Tail County was named Pelican Lake, and the surface of the water was often thick with the white birds. The large, silent birds, known only to give grunts now and then, would become a common sight in their new home with Pelican Rapids, Pelican River, and Pelican Lake all paying tribute.

Someone with a more flamboyant reputation visited the Pelican Rapids area in 1871. The soon-to-be notorious Lord Gordon Gordon was reported to have bought twenty-six sections of land and was planning a large Scotch colony.[21] (Gordon, who conferred the title "Lord" on himself, was being sought for questioning regarding a jewelry heist in England.) Gordon proposed to call the town Loomis, after John J. Loomis, land commissioner of the Northern Pacific Railroad. The Lord had become friends with Loomis, who had shown him the land in the north of Otter Tail County. The swindler persuaded landowners to "deed him interest in the townsite." He promised to colonize this area with thousands of his frugal but skilled tenants from Scotland. When none of the smooth-talking Scotsman's promises materialized, the town suffered economic and personal losses. The founder of the mill and dam, W.G. Tuttle, left town in 1876 as a broken man, who died in an insane asylum in New York.[22] Gordon had swindled bigger fish than those of Otter Tail County, including Jay Gould, president of the Erie Railway Company. It might have been considered fair play because Gould himself had issued worthless stock in the railroad and swindled scores of investors. The Coles no doubt caught a glimpse of the foreigner in town. In a 1915 footnote to her mother's account, Georgina Cole talks about the town's name:

> I want to add that Aunt Mary has an 'album quilt' which was pieced for her in 1871 by the residents of Pelican Rapids and vicinity, before the name of the town was positively determined. It was first called 'Loomis,' and on those blocks appear most the names mentioned above, giving their address as Loomis, Minnesota, also the date.

When the town was platted in 1872, it was named Pelican Rapids. The local lore records Lord Gordon as being arrested in Manitoba and committing suicide with "a pistol ball through his head."[23] Obviously the Coles did not fall prey to the slick Lord G. Gordon, for their land remained in their hands. They farmed that claim for thirty years, but they were not at first enthusiastic about making it their homestead.

Sarah's disappointment in the spot they were to call home is evident:

> It was then I felt decidedly blue: so did my husband, but we braced ourselves by saying, 'We are in for it now for sure, and we'll stay until we can get out, then we'll skip.' In the meantime we must get busy. I think the first piece of work was to go to Alexandria and take out homestead papers, a journey of over forty miles, on horseback.

The part about "skipping" is puzzling. Was the task of "carving a home out of the wilderness" more than they had bargained for? Were they disappointed in the land itself? What were their plans for farming? It could have been dispiriting to have left a settled valley of apple trees and crops and have to hack through trees over marshy land to find a place to live. Most likely, the men headed on horseback for the Stage Road to Alexandria to file their claims, under the Homestead Act, signed by President Lincoln in 1862, the same year he signed the Emancipation Proclamation. Settlers could claim up to 160 acres of public land by paying $10. However, they were obligated to work their claim for five years. If Sarah considered this as a temporary home, she must have seen five years as a long stretch.

Perhaps getting there, not being there, had been the best part for Sarah. She mentioned that she considered the journey itself a "picnic." Living in a wagon in the wilderness with a one-year-old in a Minnesota summer could not have been an idyllic campout. But they were ready, or resigned, to take their chances here; this was it. They had not left their Wisconsin home and traveled for six weeks to give up now. With the land rush in full swing, they acted from an urgency to settle a claim while acres were available. Yet even with these pioneer anxieties and uncertainties, her optimism and love of the natural setting comes through:

> Our cattle roamed the woods, and it took much time getting them home at night, and our pony was important in this. Sometimes it would be very late at night before they arrived, causing us anxiety, and I would sit by our camp fire with a big denim apron with which I shielded the baby from the mosquitoes, (and I could not see the stars only as the wind swayed the tree-tops), listening for the tinkle of our cow-bell. I often sat alone this way until late, really enjoying the wildness of it and peeping at the stars for company.

## June 19 and 20, 1998

We stayed for two nights; the first night, Friday night, was spent at the Pelican Motel, next to the Pelican Rapids Water Plant and not far from the turkey processing plant. We had arrived on the weekend of the International Friendship Festival. The motel would be full Saturday night, so we made reservations at a B&B out by Prairie Lake.

We ate our Friday night dinner at Auntie Ev's, where we decided to order from the menu rather than have the buffet. We watched as the cook came out and scooped our dinner orders off the buffet line. After dinner, we drove past the city park where a huge cement pelican stood on a wooden platform extending into the river. I felt as if I had come home; a sense of being in familiar surroundings clung to me during the visit. The names of Prairie Lake, Lake Lida, and Lake Lizzie were like old tunes from childhood. My eyes had filled with tears as we entered town. They had reached it; we had reached it.

Since I first considered following the wagons, Pelican Rapids had been my destination. It wasn't theirs. Those hard historical facts, which were recited in family stories, did not come about from thoughtful decision-making. Much of what I knew of the Cole story occurred because of their wrong turns, indecisions, or resignation. Pelican was not their promised land, but it became their cherished home. And driving through town the night before, I felt it was mine, too.

I was beginning to realize that the Coles would always be elusive, always ahead of us on the trail. We couldn't really catch up to them, even in the cemetery when we read their gravestones. Their lives were their own, their decisions and actions sprang from sources I could never explore. However, I had the descendant's advantage in knowing how it all came out. (Except for Sarah and George's oldest son, Evander Leonard Cole, called "Bud" by the family. His parents lived through his death in 1919, when he was killed in a deer-hunting accident in Michigan's Upper Peninsula.) They never knew that their youngest child, Daniel Shell Cole, my grandfather, would die in a state mental hospital, committed by his wife who had grown afraid of his manic episodes. He was transformed from a popular small-town good citizen to a man controlled by paranoia, a man who slept with a gun under his pillow. He died a few months later from a heart attack. An undiagnosed heart problem, restricting blood flow to the brain, may have contributed to his mental state.

Sometime during the busy Saturday, we stopped on U.S. Highway 59 outside of town at another historical marker, this one commemorating the discovery of "Minnesota Woman," first called "Minnesota Man," before the sex of the skeleton was determined. The young woman's bones were unearthed by a highway crew in 1931 while making a cut for a roadbed. The bones were under eight feet of silt from an extinct lake. Some archaeologists believe her to be from the Paleo-Indian period, about 6000 BC; others put her in the later Archaic period. Whatever her age, she makes the settlers of 1871 newcomers. The Cole wagons most likely rolled over her burial site as they began homesteading on Prairie Lake.

When Norm went out for breakfast, I stayed behind with a box of granola bars, did my back exercises, and shaved my legs. As I did so, I thought about Minnesota Woman and how she never shaved her legs. For that matter, neither did Sarah. The idea would have mystified, if not appalled, her. For most of her life, Sarah's legs were under a long dress. However, by the time she died in 1922, women were wearing short dresses and baring their legs.

The first International Friendship Festival was in full swing when we checked out of the motel and drove the short distance into town. Lime-green T-shirts were being sold everywhere to commemorate this "first" in Pelican's history. I picked up a schedule of summer events, which were many for a town with a population of 1,886; I saw we'd miss the Ugly Truck Contest and the Turkey Festival, both held in July, as well as the parade and fireworks. We left the crowded sidewalks and walked down to the river's edge to view the "World's Largest Pelican." Two Vietnamese girls were taking each other's pictures in front of the eighteen-foot-high bird, which was erected in 1957. It looked onto the torrent of water coming over the Mill Pond Dam on the river. It is inevitable that a town named Pelican Rapids with the Pelican River flowing through its business district would have a giant pelican. Norm and I waited while the smiling girls took numerous shots. We stood at Minnesota Bridge 5025 where it crosses the Pelican River, which flows north. Beyond the dam is another bridge, a 250-foot suspension bridge built in 1975, which links the E.L. Peterson Memorial Park and the Sherin Memorial Park, where the town's swimming pool is located.

We walked back to the main street where townspeople were standing on the sidewalks, coffee cups in hand. The first event on the festival schedule was an "international coffee break," where everyone brought their own mug and tried out coffees and "goodies" from all over the globe. We were mugless, so we turned our attention to the Vietnamese Dragon Dance. Two gaudy fabric dragons, one guy under the head and one under the tail of each, undulated down the street and onto the sidewalk, pushing the crowd out of the way with mock intimidation. A taunter with a round mask teased the dragons as they snaked between parked cars and back out onto the street. Young Vietnamese males, some of them clashing cymbals and beating drums, accompanied the procession. The dragons bobbed and swerved as multicolored capes flowed from the big papier-mâché-like heads, with bulging, popping eyes resembling Christmas tree ornaments. The traffic on Broadway Street came to a standstill.

Browsing through the stores, we lingered in a clothing shop. I asked the man behind the counter what had drawn the Vietnamese to Pelican Rapids. The answer was the turkey plant. "They like that kind of thing. You know they're in St. Cloud. They like to work with chickens and turkeys," he said.

If the turkeys brought the Vietnamese, I wondered if that was also the attraction for the Mexican people I'd seen here. There were food booths set up in the park with offerings of Vietnamese, Mexican, German, Scandinavian, and American cuisine. I was suspicious of authentic Vietnamese and Mexican food in Pelican Rapids, Minnesota, suspecting that the newcomers have had to compromise with the ingredients. We decided to pass on the booth food and have lunch at the Rapids Restaurant, a "fine dining" establishment.

We were discovering that "fine dining" was a relative term. The interior was murky, with a haze floating above the heads of the patrons. Now we wished we'd stayed outside, eating from paper plates while standing on the sidewalk. The Rapids Restaurant didn't believe in "no smoking" sections. We were surrounded by smokers—young and old. Saturday's specials were chicken dumplings and beer cheese. The chef salad was iceberg lettuce and strips of Velveeta. (What would Sarah have thought of Velveeta?) When we wobbled back out into the bright June day, I felt we'd been subjected to a string of unhealthy experiences, from which our cholesterol levels and lungs would not soon recover. However, we'd probably been exposed to a more truly authentic Pelican eating experience than if we'd eaten food from the festival booths.

After lunch we walked over to the tourist center, where I bought *A Century at the Rapids* (1883–1983). We learned that the old Frazee house on East Mill was now owned by the Kings, who had opened it for a holiday tour and would probably be glad to show it to us. I wanted to buy a copy of *75 Years of Progress 1883–1958* (*Pelican Rapids Diamond Jubilee June 22–24*), but there were none. We were told the library had a copy. The library was a hopping place—a line at the copy machine and a steady stream of people checking out books. Norm found an 1884 plat book and looked up the farmland owned by the Coles. We spent a small fortune in change at the copy machine. I xeroxed the page from the seventy-fifth anniversary book with Sarah and George's photos. They are probably in their sixties, both handsome people, wearing rimless spectacles. Sarah has dark, distinct eyebrows and clear eyes. Her wide mouth turns down. Her wavy white hair is pulled back. George has a mustache and a full head of hair. The blurb beside their pictures says that "the trip was made in forty days ..." *Forty days* gave a new dimension to their emigration. I had been looking at it as six weeks, but standing there at the copy machine, I compared the three wagons of Coles to a band of Israelites wandering in the desert.

A Mexican mariachi band was going to play in the park in the afternoon, with an evening concert at the Maplewood Veterans Hospital. But we had more searching to do. The Coles seemed to exist on two planes: camping out by Prairie Lake as they cleared the land—and resting in the cemetery just outside town.

When Norm had gone to breakfast at Aunt Ev's, he had returned with a paper napkin full of directions to five cemeteries. As we headed for the Pelican Valley Cemetery on the south of town, I thought of the bones under the ground. Reading about the "Minnesota Woman" had given me an appreciation for all the populations who had lived their lives on Minnesota soil.

That afternoon of our first full day in Pelican, we entered the land of ancestors, mine and everyone else's. That night I wrote:

> *We spent several hours walking through cemeteries from our directions on the napkin: Ringsaker, Norwegian Grove, North Immanuel Lutheran, Pelican Valley and Lakeview. Most were crowded with Norwegians, the inscriptions in Norwegian. At the Pelican Valley Cemetery, an old windmill creaks and whines. A mobile home settlement in one direction, fields in the other. At the last cemetery— Lakeview—I found what I'd been looking for: Coles, Frazees, DePochees. I want to clip the grass and place flowers there, especially at Sarah's stone. Perhaps I can at least pick wildflowers. A golf course (Birchwood) borders the cemetery, with low fencing to keep the balls out of the grave area ...*

Though I knew Sarah died in 1922, seeing her grave confirmed the end of her journey in Minnesota, and in life. It also affirmed my journey in following her here. She'd been waiting for me. At the end of that warm summer day, the voices of golfers floated over the graveyard. The grass was long around the edges of the stones. Wishing I had some clippers with me, I pulled up what I could by hand. Her grave needed flowers; only orange-rust lichen blossomed there. I was an unprepared guest. The chiseled letters were still easy to read:

### SARAH M.
### WIFE OF
### GEO. W. COLE
### APR. 20, 1845-JUNE 28, 1922

### TAUGHT AT THE FIRST SCHOOL
### IN PELICAN RAPIDS

One of several obituaries, this one from the Fergus Falls Weekly Journal, described her death:

> *She had been out walking and was stricken suddenly, presumably with apoplexy. She fell and was picked up and carried to her home where she expired in a few minutes. She was 75 years of age and was enjoying her usual health, and had attended the Old Settler's picnic at Battle Lake Sunday.*

According to my Aunt Ruth, Sarah had decided to walk to a wedding, only a quarter of a mile away. She and George were then living in a house in town. She sat down beside the road to rest and passed out. The obituary incorrectly reported her age. She was 77, and up until then, her health had been good. However, George had been plagued with disabling rheumatism for years.

With plans to return to the cemetery the next morning to spend more time with the Coles, we drove out County Road 9 to the Prairie View Estate B&B, located on a farm once owned by a Norwegian bachelor farmer, obviously tidier than many of Garrison Keillor's depictions. The carpets were unworn, the woodwork and doors original. The three bedrooms were comfy and not overly decorated like so many B&Bs. Phyllis Haugrud and her two sisters were the current owners. Their uncle, the Norwegian bachelor farmer, left them eight hundred acres along with the house and buildings. We looked at the 1884 plat map and saw that Phyllis's great-grandfather, an Extad, owned land adjoining several Cole parcels. Her family extended their land holdings, while the Coles sold out. Why? By comparing the 1884 and a 1983 plat map, we realized that we would be sleeping on land once owned by Coles. In 1884 Karl Cole, William Henry's oldest, owned this particular piece. I was a bit miffed at the Coles—and envious of Phyllis, whose life was connected to the land of her ancestors. She and her husband hunted up a 1925 plat book for us. Nary a Cole on any property by then. Were they lousy farmers? Did they grab the first chance for a job in town? The 1983 plat map showed Lone Acres Turkey Farms where Sarah and George and their relatives once homesteaded.

Since it was a Saturday night, I broke my rule for no TV or radio to listen to *A Prairie Home Companion*. No other guests had arrived. Norm and I shared a bottle of wine as we listened to the program with our door to the hallway open. Later Phyllis told us she had gone to a packed-out event where Keillor was the speaker. After a couple of glasses of Chardonnay, I felt a part of the prairie; I was ready to go down to the dining room table for a tuna hot dish, Jell-O salad, and bars. Instead, because this was a B&B, we headed over to the Pelican Supper Club.

The parking lot of the supper club was jammed with cars. The building was a huge pole barn, an example of contemporary prairie architecture, and much less substantial looking than the log-hewn buildings of the pioneers. Inside, half of the space was devoted to a bar and karaoke area, which was being used for a raucous wedding reception. The other wing was the dining room, with the ever-present salad bar. (Why chocolate pudding and marshmallow whip sit next to lettuce and carrot sticks is one of the great mysteries of the twentieth century.) The tables held from four to twelve people. I expected to be seated at a table with others, but we were shown to an empty table. Maybe we looked like out-of-towners who weren't going to order Old Milwaukee and ribs.

The din from the wedding party drifted into the dining area. We ordered walleye in a sea of steak eaters. It arrived undercooked and pallid, as if embarrassed to be seen.

At 9:30 p.m. it was still light, a soft glow filling the sky as we drove back to the B&B. We braked when we saw another cemetery. This one, called Bethany, was filled with Norwegians. It was small, and a quick tour told us there were no Coles here.

That night in the high bed in the farmhouse, I thought of the two weddings—the one with a raucous reception at the Supper Club and the one to which Sarah had been heading when death stopped her. It was fitting that she died on the way to a celebration, that she died still participating in the affairs of Pelican.

I dreamed of moving to western Minnesota. Norm and I would buy an old farmhouse by Prairie Lake and renovate it. I'd write, surrounded by my ancestors, and become known as that woman who moved here to be around her dead relatives. I'd sell copies of Sarah's account to tourists.

# CAMPING OUT—AND FOOD

## *Summer 1871*

*We had plenty of milk all along, and while on the road set it in pans on the ground at night, each covered with another pan. In the morning I would pour off the cream into a 5-gallon churn which we found room for in the front corner of the wagon, and during the day it churned itself into little balls the size of a hazel-nut, so we had nice butter too. We had an old-fashioned tin baking oven and could bake delicious biscuits by our camp fires.*

—Sarah Moore Leonard Cole

The Coles I've known have always been ardent campers, perhaps out of necessity. But I think there is an ingrained love of being outdoors and preparing and eating food. I have it; my mother has it; as did her father, Daniel Cole, Sarah and George's youngest. When my mother was a girl, the family trips from Michigan to Minnesota were made with the heavy canvas tent. Of course, there were no motels, so camping was not uncommon.

The permanent campsite near Prairie Lake from June to October in 1871 must have been the scene of some delicious meals. The fish were plentiful, and there were biscuits from the tin oven. They had ducks, hens, and cows to contribute to the menu. However, fresh vegetables, other than potatoes, were not plentiful. They could have picked wild berries as the summer continued.

The families of George and William Cole spent the summer of 1871 as campers, while the elders were housed in an existing shack. Was there music and storytelling at the end of the day? I like to imagine them singing around a campfire, with one of them playing the old family fiddle. Or were they too worn out from clearing the land? The daily chores were relentless; they may have longed for their snug houses back in the Lemonweir Valley.

59

The overturned bureau with its stack of quilts was Sarah and George's bed. Little Georgie may have slept in a drawer or basket. After the smoke from the campfire had died away, did Minnesota's legendary carnivorous mosquitoes plague them during the night? The three women, Sarah, Hannah, and Mary (and perhaps a fourth if Aunt Liz was along), would have agreed on a domestic protocol in the wilderness. The picture of the three families congregating for communal meals is appealing, but there must have been much negotiating among these strong-minded women in coming up with a list of duties and responsibilities. Sarah was on the receiving end of advice from her mother-in-law, who had been through the pioneering experience before. Her sister-in-law, older than she as well as being the mother of five, filled the role as mentor to Sarah, a new mother.

There is a family story about difficulties between Sarah and her mother-in-law later on. The way my Aunt Beth remembers it, Hannah and another relative of her generation (perhaps a Cocking woman) had started drinking their own urine, apparently for medicinal reasons. The three women were in the same house; Sarah expressed her disgust at their practice and stalked out.

In a tastier vein, Aunt Ruth passed on some recipes including one for cupcakes. It's possible these could have been baked in the tin oven over the campfire beside Prairie Lake.

*Grandma Sarah Cole Cup Cakes*
*1 c. sugar*
*Butter-size egg*
*1 c. sour milk*
*1 tsp. soda*
*2 tsp. lt. molasses*
*2 c. flour*
*½ tsp. nutmeg*
*½ tsp. cinnamon*
*pinch salt*

This recipe does not appear in the December 1915 *Pelican Rapids Cook Book*. In fact, the only contribution by Sarah is a recipe for catsup. The cookbook came out the same year her account of pioneer experiences was published by the *St. Paul Farmers' Dispatch*. She may have been busy with her writing and unable to meet the deadline for submitting recipes. I see her in 1915 concocting a batch of catsup, using the onions, tomatoes, horseradish, and peppers from her garden—a cultivated space that was wilderness in 1871.

*Cold Tomato Catsup*
*1½ pts. cider vinegar, ½ c salt, 1 c sugar, ½ c mustard seed, 1 oz. celery seed, 1*
*tsp. cloves, 1 tsp. mace, 2 tsp. cinnamon, 2 tsp. black pepper, 3 onions chopped fine,*
*3 ripe large green peppers, 1 c grated horse radish, ½ pk. chopped ripe tomatoes.*
*This will keep in open jars.*
*Mrs. George Cole*

## *Camping in My Life*

When I first started planning this trip, I envisioned pitching a tent and camping out. At one point, I considered duplicating Sarah's trip and traveling by wagon, but the logistics involved in such a journey brought me to my senses. I realized what I really wanted was to see her trip juxtaposed with twentieth-century technology (i.e., my car). I was intimidated a bit by camping alone in new territory. Before I remarried, I thought of having my dog as my wagon trail buddy. But when Norm entered the picture as enthusiastic companion and not-so-ardent camper, the tent stayed in the closet. Instead we encountered uncomfortable beds and home cooking that we wished had stayed at home. My temperamental back complained after nights on sagging beds. I envied Sarah her hard sleeping surface on the bureau. I longed for her biscuits and real butter. I'd always spurned margarine as a child. My sisters considered me an elitist. "Marla has to have *real* butter." I was taken with the art of making butter after seeing it made at a neighbor's house when I was a child. Reading Sarah's account of how they got their butter generated another poem, also published by *The Christian Science Monitor*:

*Recipe for Butter*
*Set out pans beside the wagon,*
*Cover milk against the night.*

*Dawn reveals a yellow layer*
*Pulled to the top by lunar light.*

*Pour off cream into the churn,*
*Anchor it in the wagon's front.*
*Harvest the fruits of a rough ride*
*Butterballs big as hazelnuts.*

*Marla Kay Houghteling*

Sarah and George's youngest child, Daniel, was a dedicated camper. He was my mother's father and she told of family outings, trying to erect the heavy canvas tent with its myriad poles. There are photos of young Dan and his wife, Grace Cocking Cole, sitting in front of a tent. Their honeymoon was spent camping near Pelican, at Lake Lizzy or Lake Lida. In the photos, Grace is always in a dress; Dan wears a slouchy cap and rough clothes. Later, he grew to love canoeing Michigan's rivers, especially the White and Pere Marquette. Both he and his older brother Evander were avid outdoorsmen. A newspaper article tells of twelve-year-old Evander (or "Bud") on a trip down the Pelican River in a birchbark canoe. On this trip, Bud managed the bow paddle and a shotgun. The party of four navigated the river through several rapids, past hay meadows, and through canebrake and wild rice.

The family trips of my childhood in the 1950s, navigated in a Mercury station wagon from Michigan to Florida, were similar to wagon accommodations. (Although I can't imagine anyone actually sleeping in a moving wagon.) My youngest sister was wrapped in a cocoon of blankets on the ledge of the back window. The middle sister had the seat, and I had the floor. My father positioned a long board over the hump. Several folded quilts provided a mattress. I loved sleeping there, only inches from the pavement. The hum of the tires was a lullaby, and I slept with the security of being in a confined space with my family in the dead of night, traveling through states I'd never seen. Perhaps it was my love affair with traveling that sparked the strong connection I felt with Sarah the first time I read her words.

My parents did not have a love affair with tents. I remember one or two summer vacations spent in a damp tent, playing Fish or Old Maid while the relentless rain hammered the canvas. Next my parents tried a pop-up—part camper trailer, part tent. Finally they reached the RV stage and never looked back at sleeping on or near the ground.

But I have developed into a tent person. Camping has been a part of summer since my twenties. The campgrounds of today, with restrooms, showers, ice, and firewood would astound the Coles. When I couldn't take a camping trip, I pitched the tent in the backyard. I'm grateful when I think how much easier and lighter it is to camp with my nylon dome tent than with Dan Cole's cumbersome canvas affair with its heavy wood poles.

The night of my fiftieth birthday I slept in my L.L. Bean tent with my dog beside me on her own sleeping bag. I had moved to northern Michigan six months before and was renting a little house on a hill. My mother, my sisters, and their families had come up north for my birthday party. They all slept inside, but I wanted to start my fiftieth year outside under the sky.

Now after encountering "deep valley" motel mattresses, sleeping on the hard surface of a bureau sounds like the height of comfort. My demanding back, minus two disks, appreciates a good firm surface. My own traveling involves checking out mattresses in several motel rooms in order to find the firmest. I often carry a sleeping bag when visiting friends who outfit their beds with hammock-like mattresses. After I say good night, I hit the floor.

As for the food during our June trip along the wagon trail—Norm and I didn't encounter real butter or homemade biscuits. We did eat "homemade" raspberry pie, which turned out to be pinkish Jell-O in a board-hard shell. And there was the walleye that had been microwaved into horror-movie whiteness and texture. It almost made me hunger for the potatoes planted when the Coles first arrived at Prairie Lake—potatoes that "one could carry ... on the arm like stove wood."

# AMONG THE DEAD

## *June 21, 1998*

We returned to Lakeview Cemetery on a quiet Sunday morning. Voices from the driving range drifted over through the spitting rain. Tent-like in an army surplus rain poncho, I wandered among the stones, writing dates and names on damp paper. Norm took pictures while I wrote. We were peaceful and satisfied: Phyllis had served us strawberry waffles for breakfast. A car pulled up into the drive and a woman got out, carrying fresh flowers, and walked to the newer section of the cemetery.

There were lots of Cady tombstones. William Henry Cole married Mary Elizabeth Cady. (I wondered if there was any connection to Elizabeth Cady Stanton.) I still hadn't found William's grave. The small stones or markers for children and babies tinged my meanderings with sadness. Those who traveled in two of the three wagons from Wisconsin in 1871 were here. The elder Coles, Levi and Hannah, were memorialized down to the day: *Aged 73 yrs. 2 mos. 25 days* for Levi and *Aged 73 yrs. 2 mos. 3 days* for Hannah. The gravestones of the next two generations did not provide as much detail. Rather there was an indication of their affiliations. George Washington Cole's grave bore the compass and square symbols of the Freemasons. There was no GAR marker. He would have been only fifteen when the Civil War started. Sarah's inscription identified her as a wife and a pioneering teacher.

Two of their four children, the daughters, were here. Both sons were buried in Michigan, where they had made their homes and careers. Georgina, the oldest, died in 1943. She was the "baby in the wagon" who turned one on June 6, 1871, the date of their arrival in Pelican Rapids. In 1916, at the age of forty-six, she married Wilson Harris, from another Pelican pioneer family. There was nothing to be learned from her simple stone. I'm fortunate that she was a prolific letter writer because much of the information about the Coles comes from her. My aunts, Tillie's nieces, inherited the letter-writing gene as well as the inclination to save family letters. To whom will I pass on all these women's letters? Will my nieces or nephew be interested in them? In the age of email and phone answering machines, these "snail mail" documents seem even more precious.

Flora Matilda, born in 1878, was called Tillie. On July 4, 1900, she married Paul Clifford Frazee, whose family ran established businesses in oil and flour mills. It was the name Frazee City, read in promotional literature by her elders, that had lured the Coles to Minnesota. Tillie settled into a life in Pelican until after her husband's death in 1936, when she moved to Colorado, supposedly for health reasons.

Aunt Tillie was the one from this generation of Coles who I knew best, although I never met her. I corresponded with my great-aunt for about ten years when I was growing up. I remember the degree of respect I felt. We wrote to each other as equals. I'd heard the family stories about Aunt Tillie. My mother had always referred to Tillie as a Christian Scientist, but more recently she's said her aunt was probably a "Mental Scientist," which I think was a term for a follower of Scientology. She must have embraced this religion in the 1950s. I remember my Aunt Ruth giving me a book on Dianetics by L. Ron Hubbard when I went to college. Perhaps both women shared an interest in this twentieth-century religion.

Tillie, like Georgina, was a firm believer in keeping the historical record accurate and up-to-date. She supported the efforts of the local historical societies back in Minnesota. At the Otter Tail County Historical Society, I discovered a regular flow of letters to Fergus Falls from Denver.

During World War II, while my father was stationed with the army in Colorado, my mother and her first child, my older sister, lived with Aunt Tillie. They were back in Michigan when she wrote to them in July of 1945.

*I am thinking of you often, and much of the time—Have intended to write again, and before this, but other things have interfered. Both Mr. and Mrs. Kaltenbach, and Mrs. L. too, have expressed their sympathy. Mrs. Hagen is going to have a baby before long, so nothing has been said to her about it. She has kept very much to herself for months—I have scarcely seen her until within a week, have seen her hanging some clothes on the line.*

Aunt Tillie is referring to the death of their baby. My father had broken his kneecap while helping push a stalled car on a Denver street. After months in Fitzsimmons Hospital, he was discharged from the army. My parents moved back to Michigan, where soon after their daughter, only sixteen months, died. Aunt Tillie continued:

*I keep wondering what you will do now. Would you like to come back to Colorado? Or will you take a position again somewhere? Am sure a change of some kind will be best for you. Of course, if Jack has a good job and one that is congenial, it may not be best to change your abode, but if you had work outside your home, it seems to me it would be good for you. Write when you can and tell me your plans, won't you?*

Tillie's advice is not what I would have expected. She had five children and after marriage had not "worked outside the home," as far as I know. Perhaps her views had changed as she grew older. Perhaps the idea of work was the only thing she had to comfort her niece, mourning the death of her first child.

A more carefree image of my great-aunt Tillie comes into focus with an anecdote from my Aunt Beth, her niece. While growing up on Prairie Lake, Tillie loved to fish and would use frogs as bait. She carried the frogs in the puffy sleeves of her dress.

She died in 1969 while I was in West Africa with the Peace Corps. I regret not saving her letters to me. Here in the cemetery, she is beside her husband, not Tillie Cole, but Flora M., wife of Paul C. Frazee.

I had experienced an overwhelming peace during the two days of wandering through cemeteries. Cremation and the scattering of ashes had always appealed to me as a means of recycling one's remains and maintaining an ongoing connection with the cosmos—"dust to dust." Now I was beginning to appreciate graves. A graveyard provided an address. The stone, the names, the dates, the epitaphs kept the dead connected to the living and provided comfort—and information.

Evander W. Leonard, Sarah's father, was buried nearby. His dates were not as clear, but it looked like 1818 to 1880. Like George's grave, this one had a Masonic emblem. There was no evidence of his wife's grave, Sarah's stepmother. The father who had warned her about uprooting herself from Wisconsin soil had himself moved to Minnesota.

Two flat stones were covered by grass and dirt. I cleared off the surfaces to find the graves of her brother, Melvin Leonard (1843–1922), who was in the Civil War (Co. F. 35th Vol. Inf. GAR); and of Sarah J. (1851–1945), who must have been Melvin's wife. (The popularity of the names Sarah and Mary make it difficult to keep the generations straight.) Melvin died the same year as his sister Sarah. His wife Sarah lived on for two more decades. Sarah Cole's life was richer when her father and brother emigrated:

> My optimistic letters to my relatives in Wisconsin and the desire to see us brought my father to visit us twice before 1878, and about that time he decided to join us in the new country, sold out in Wisconsin, and both he and my brother came also to take up land near Pelican Rapids, my father establishing a drug store in the town. This brought much happiness to me, and I felt I could ask for nothing more. The way we entertained them in our log cabin of two rooms that first winter they were with us would furnish material for another story, but is too long to write here.

The most ornate gravestone, banked by a bed of pink peonies, bore the name DePochee. It towered over the individual plain stones embedded in the earth for each family member. George Washington Cole's older sister, Mary Elizabeth (1838–1917), the wife of Louis DePochee, was here. I assumed Mary must have come out to Minnesota *after* 1871, until I came across her obituary from the *Fergus Falls Journal* at the Otter Tail County Historical Society the next day, and was filled in on more Cole family history:

> She was born at West Troy, N.Y. November 25, 1838, and when but six years of age came west with her parents, Levi Cole and Hannah C. Van Arnam Cole, to settle near Mauston, Wisconsin, from whence they emigrated to Minnesota in 1870 [1871], and took up land near Pelican Rapids. She was married to Louis DePochee, a veteran of the Civil [W]ar, August 24, 1874, at Fergus Falls, Minnesota. ... Mary Van Arnam Cole DePochee was a lineal descendant of James Cole of Plymouth, Mass. (1633) who came from England and acquired the land on which Plymouth Rock stands and for whom the adjacent hill, known as

*'Cole's Hill,' was named. She was also a descendant of Levi P. Cole who served as assistant master-at-arms on the frigate Providence during the Revolution, under Commodore Whipple; and of Abram Van Arnam, one of the founders of Northville, N.Y. (1800) ...*

So Mary must have been in the wagon with the elder Coles. Apparently a single woman at the time of emigration, she later married Louis DePochee, credited with being Lida Township's first settler in 1871. After her marriage at 36, she had two sons, one of whom died in infancy.

Her obituary mentioned that a letter written by her the day before she died was received in Pelican Rapids. The town newspaper printed the following passage. It is unclear whether this piece was actually written by Mary or whether she included it in her letter—or whether it was a public tribute.

> *Wasn't it pleasant, oh, brother mine,*
> *In those old days of the lost sunshine*
> *Of youth—when the Saturday's chores were through*
> *And the 'Sunday wood' in the kitchen, too,*
> *And we went visiting, 'me and you,'*
> *Out to Old Aunt Mary's!*
>
> *It all comes back clear today!*
> *Though I am old and you are gray*
> *We patter along in the dust again,*
> *Out by the barn-lot, and down the lane,*
> *As light as the tips of the drops of rain,*
> *Out to Old Aunt Mary's!*
>
> *And, oh, my brother, so far away,*
> *This is to tell you she waits today*
> *To welcome us—Aunt Mary fell*
> *Asleep this morning, whispering—Tell*
> *The boys to come! And all is well*
> *Out to Old Aunt Mary's.*

More Sunday golfers had arrived at the neighboring course, unaware that a family reunion was going on at Lakeview Cemetery. As we left, I experienced a Sunday morning benediction, the blessings of my ancestors as I made my way through the world. I got into the car beside Norm, cloaked in the security of being part of a large clan. That day I walked above them, but one day I would be a citizen of the past, too.

# PLATES

*Sarah and George Cole, in later life*

*Georgina Cole (the baby in the wagon) with her younger brother, Daniel—around 1894*

*Merton Eberlein, Mauston,*
*Wisconsin's historiographer*

*Fort Snelling*

*Marla at Pomme de Terre*

*Sarah's grave—"Taught the first school in Pelican Rapids"*

*Levi Cole's grave*

*One of the more recent pioneers in Pelican Rapids*

*Vietnamese festival in downtown Pelican*

*Marla meets Mildred Frazee, a living link to the Coles in Pelican (Tillie Cole Frazee's daughter-in-law)*

*Cole family: Standing left to right: Georgina, Evander, Tillie. Front row left to right: Sarah, Daniel, George*

*The Toyota Camry turns 100,000 on the way home to Michigan*

*Marla and Norm, building their own home in the wilderness*

# THE RIGHT SPOT

## June 1871

*The river runs through a chain of 12 lakes, large and small, and we located on the east side of the lake nearest the village site, called Prairie Lake, about two miles northeast of the village. The brothers took homesteads adjoining—we could take up only 80 acres each, and we had to ford the river at the lake's outlet, cut down trees, and literally carve a roadway to our claims, and even then our chicken coops got torn off, but the chickens and ducks serenely followed the wagons.*

—Sarah Moore Leonard Cole

## June 21, 1998

Our next stop after the cemetery was Prairie Lake, where it connected with the Pelican River. On this Sunday, the tall reeds lining the edges of the water reminded me of the Bible story of Moses hidden in his basket in the bulrushes. No one was in the bulrushes today. We had the spot to ourselves. The lake and river were calm, their surfaces rippled now and then by a breeze that rattled the reeds. The Coles had forded the river to get to their claims, not far from here. I was standing on a spot on the planet Earth where Sarah had stood. From the dock that was now a part of a public access, I read aloud Sarah's description of how they reached their land. Norm fell off a guardrail while trying to get a high shot of me by the lake's outlet. He skinned his shin and hand—and banged up his camera. After commiserating with him, I wondered about all the scrapes, bruises, and cuts my ancestors accumulated in clearing the forest.

After Prairie Lake, we drove out U.S. Highway 59 to County Road 4. About a mile up the road was an abandoned schoolhouse. Going by the 1884 plat map, it could have been the school, or one of the schools, where Sarah taught. It wasn't far from Cole land. We walked around the old building, a sad, compelling place with its smell of dry rot and the tall, tall grasses. It was pleasant to stand there and fantasize about buying the property and renovating the building, perhaps turning it into a summer retreat. The next day at the Otter Tail County Museum, we would see a photographic display of rural schools. The three in Pelican Township were:

District 18 Oak Grove, organized Oct. 3, 1870; dissolved 1951; converted to private residence.

District 79 Dandy Views School, organized Jan. 2, 1871; dissolved 1961; abandoned.

District 26 Holen School, organized Nov. 17, 1871; dissolved 1951; converted to private residence.

Our bet was on the Dandy Views School as the one where Sarah had taught.

We continued on past Lake Lida and Lake Crystal, seeing signs for Lake Lizzie. We stopped and picked up a brochure from one of the Lake Lida resorts, plain wooden cabins strung along the lakeshore. Perhaps one day we'd be back.

I realized it was Father's Day. Norm was here in Minnesota with me; his two grown children lived on the East Coast. I treated him to lunch at the Dairy Queen, where the woman behind the counter gave us the name of a man out on State Highway 108 who might know who owned the old schoolhouse. Here was yet another in our long list of friendly, helpful people. I wasn't sure if this was a lead worth pursuing, but I was warmed by the Pelicanites connections with their town's history.

I had phoned Mildred Frazee before we left the B&B. We set up a visit for the afternoon. She told me she went to church, had lunch, and shopped with some other women—her Sunday routine. I remembered seeing her gravestone at Lakeview this morning. Her husband Paul R. Frazee's name was followed by two dates: 1904–1984. The stone next to it was incomplete: Mildred H. 1909–

Mildred was waiting for us in the lobby of Pelican's "high rise," devoted to seniors. Her apartment overlooked the mill pond, whose history is linked to the Frazee flour mills. I tried to imagine living my whole life in a small town, where the past is always woven into the present, where it has to be confronted daily. Having lived in several locales, I've had the luxury of reinventing myself.

At 89, Mildred was trim and attractive. She told us she had broken both hips and had one replaced. Now she usually left her cane at home. She walked with ease as we followed her into her comfortable apartment. After she had showed us photos of her children and grandchildren, I asked directions to Aunt Tillie's house. Oh, goodness, she said, she wasn't good with words, not good at explaining things—like directions to the house. She would take us there! Mildred seemed eager for another Sunday outing.

She sat in the front passenger seat of the Toyota and directed us. We got off the main road and approached the house on a large circular driveway. The architecture was an anomaly for Pelican Rapids, with its red-tile roof, screened-in upper porch, and sunroom. The exterior was stucco, in keeping with the tile roof, although we'd seen this tan stucco on several houses in the area. The house had passed out of the Frazee family and was now owned by the Kings. Mildred was pleased with its appearance, with the restoration done by the current owners. They had an open house during the holidays. We learned that this was Mildred's home after Tillie moved to Colorado. Mildred raised three children here, and the large house with its five bedrooms "nearly killed her."

Just down a side street, a short walk away, was the Cole house. It had gone through many changes since Sarah and George lived in it after their return from Scottville, Michigan. Both houses were bordered by the river, where the children swam. I tried to imagine Sarah walking from her house to the bank, grieving over her oldest son's death, and watching her grandchildren splashing in the river. Did she ever miss the farm? Mildred, from one of the area's Norwegian families, swam with Dorothy, Tillie's oldest daughter. The sisters-in-law were friends as young women and have stayed in touch over the years. Dorothy, older than Mildred, lives in California. Until not long ago, they talked on the phone each month. Mildred was worried because she hadn't heard from Dorothy for the past few months.

There was so much I wanted to ask Mildred, but I refrained from pumping her for family information. I just needed to get a flavor of the Coles. She didn't know Sarah and George too well. I asked her about my great-aunt Tillie, her mother-in-law. She referred to Tillie as "Grandma," who wasn't good at visiting people, but who loved to sit down at her desk and write letters. *I know*, I told her. I corresponded with Aunt Tillie when I was a girl. Mildred told us that her husband Paul had attended Carleton College and wasn't keen on going into the family business. However, that's what he ended up doing. The original Frazee house, where Clifford Frazee (Tillie's husband) had grown up, no longer existed. The hospital sits on that piece of land.

I told Mildred we stayed at the B&B. Her father had been friends with the original owner, so she was acquainted with the farm. One of Mildred's friends won a free night at the B&B during its opening and took her along. Mildred said it was the loneliest night she ever spent. One other person was staying there. They sat in the yard until it was time to go to bed. In the morning, they got up, had a cinnamon roll, and went home. As we left her at the door of her building, she said she envied us our "interesting lives." She had left "P.R." briefly to work in Seattle but had returned because of family responsibilities. That feeling was all over Pelican Rapids. Family. I was feeling it too, the pull of family from another century.

# TILLIE'S STORY

T illie (Mrs. P.C. Frazee) gave a talk for the Otter Tail County Historical Society's meeting on Nov. 7, 1936. This must have been just before she moved to Denver. Her husband had died in May, so she was a recent widow. She began by reading a portion of her mother Sarah's memoir and then continued on with her own.

*I was born in the log cabin with the puncheon floor described in the foregoing story, on the 8th of May, 1878. That morning, father picked a bunch of crabapple blossoms which he took in and laid on Mother's pillow, and I have always felt that they are my birthday flower, although more often than otherwise, they were not visible even as buds until a week or several weeks later, for spring is unusually late in Minnesota.*

*I lived within a few rods of the spot where I was born until I was married at the age of twenty two. Not being very strong, I was not sent to school until I was eight years old. I loved to be out of doors, and mother being a wise woman, encouraged me in my desire to spend most of my time about the farm with father. I think he liked my company, and I really believed I helped him.*

*He was obliged to clear heavy timber from every foot of land that he farmed. This required a great amount of labor for most of the trees were hard maple, virgin growth, and measured up to two and one half feet in diameter a short distance above the ground. He used neither dynamite nor stump puller, but felled each tree with axe and saw, cut the main trunk into cord-wood, the larger branches into stove-wood, and the rest was put into brush piles, and later these were burned where they stood. He dug and pried out the stumps by hand with axe, grub-hoe, and a long pole for a lever. I used to sit on the lever with him and think I was helping materially to pry out the stump.*

*We had no cistern in those days, only rain barrels, and when the rain water gave out, father used to haul water from the lake, about 40 rods away, for washing clothes. He had a peculiar sort of sled for this purpose fashioned by himself from the crotch of a tree, which he called a 'jimmy.' There was a clevis at the point to fasten the whiffletrees to, and a board secured by bolts, across the V, making the 'jimmy' look somewhat like a capital A with the point turned up a little. On this, he placed a rain barrel, and in the barrel he would often put me for a ride to the lake. On arriving, he would drive right in, the barrel would tip onto its side, and I would crawl out into the water. That was great fun! And of course I was prepared for it.*

*Another pleasant memory I have of those early days is of riding at the tail of the rack when grain was being stacked. No one had heard of shock threshing then. Father would place a long board or plank in the bottom of the rack, allowing it to extend out behind several feet, and on the end which came within the rack, he piled the first bundles to hold the board in place. On this projecting board, I would ride all day long, from shock to shock, getting off each time while the bundles were being pitched onto the load, and watching with the dogs at the side of the shock for mice and chipmunks. At that time, father 'cradled' and bound all the grain by hand, so it had to stand in the shock much longer than it does these days, and often there would be nests of young mice under the shocks. These were delicate morsels for our big Newfoundland dog, and he took them at a gulp, wagging his tail for more.*

*I seldom had anyone of my own age to play with, but I didn't mind very much. There were the dogs to run with, and I always found plenty to amuse me as long as I could be out of doors. Children today do not seem to be able to get pleasure out of simple things as we did then.*

Tillie's attention to detail, her descriptions of material objects are a family trait. That same detailed discussion is evident in the letters written by her older sister Georgina and older brother Evander. One can see her love of being outdoors with her father and of the parents' real concern for their child. Her comment about the children of the 1930s as compared to the children of the late 1800s has been used by every generation.

Like her mother, Tillie began teaching school at 16:

*I taught my first school when I was sixteen. Caroline S. Nygren was County Superintendent. Seventeen was the required age, but I had passed the examination, except for age, and was granted a 'Permit' to teach if I could find a school board that would hire me. I did, and so began a school 12 miles from home in October, 1894. There were 18 pupils, some larger than I and almost as old. The first morning, the largest boy handed me a note from his father, saying he didn't wish to have any complaints made to him about his boys; I must handle them myself. This was rather disconcerting, but I managed to get along. I found out later that he had a great deal of difficulty managing his boys.*

*My school house was very small and built of logs. The floor was laid crosswise of the room, and the desks and seats (home-made ones, and wonderfully carved 'by hand') were nailed to two-by-fours near the floor, so that one could not be moved without moving the whole row. Sweeping under them was a problem. There were two blackboards about 30 by 40 inches, made of 'matched' boards that didn't 'match' very well. These had been painted black, but most of the paint had worn off. Erasers were pieces of board covered with scraps of sheep pelt worn to the skin. There wasn't a piece of chalk much more than an inch long. The heater was an old box stove with a broken leg. The children informed me that it had fallen down once, and one of the boys had burned his hands holding it up until something could be found to take the place of the broken leg.*

*I walked a mile and a half to school and built my own fires and swept the floor. It was because of the poor condition of the school and the consequent difficulty they had in securing a teacher that they were willing to hire me, with only a 'Permit.' In payment for my services, I received orders on the district for $30 a month which were discounted 10 per cent when cashed.*

*My next school was better, but unusual in some respects. One thing, of no particular interest, but rather odd, I thought, was the fact that I had 4 Emmas, 3 Josephines, 3 Johns, and several with two of the same name, all in this one school. The school house was quite small, though frame, but I had an enrollment of 52 with seating capacity, two in a seat, for 32. I was obliged to tuck them where I could. The back seats were against the wall—no desks behind them. I had six on each side of me on the rostrum—three in a seat. When the children sat in the recitation seats, they would put their feet on the edge of the rostrum, they were so close. Most of the beginners sat three in a seat. The Superintendent visited me the third day of school. Needless to say, I did not get a good mark on my next certificate in 'Methods in the School Room,' but next time it was 'sky high' and I felt better.*

*This school was on the prairie, and gophers used to come into the entry, knock the covers off the children's dinner pails and filch bread and butter from them. I suggested that they hang their pails on the hooks and leave bits of bread for the gophers to find. That worked well, and before the term was out, the gophers would come in and eat from my hand as I sat on the rostrum at the front of the room while all the children were in their seats, grinning but silent.*

Tillie's teaching career ended when she married Paul Clifford Frazee in 1900. That was a memorable year for another reason: her older brother Evander Cole (named for Sarah's father, Evander Leonard) returned from Alaska.

*When I was teaching at New York Mills, in the fall of 1899, we got word that President McKinley was coming through on the Northern Pacific and that the train would slow up so that the school children might see him if they wished. We all were on hand, teachers and pupils. He came out on the rear platform of the observation car, looking just like the pictures we had seen of him, and everyone felt well pleased at having seen one of our best presidents.*

*It was here, at New York Mills, that my brother, E.L. Cole, came to see me on his return from Alaska in the spring of 1900. He had gone into that country during the 'gold rush' of 1898, over the inland or Edmonton Trail, and had returned via Glenora and Seattle. I would have given anything to be able to return home with him and hear him relate his adventures, but I had my school to finish and could not. That was the last school I taught.*

Most likely Tillie's role as wife and mother curtailed her outdoor activities, but that love of nature, of just being in the out-of-doors, was transmitted to her children. One of her sons, Ralph, moved to Oregon and for a time lived in the mountains where he raised Angora goats. A letter to his Aunt Georgie in 1938 kindly accepts her offer of a comforter for his "bachelor's quarters."

# June 22, 1998

We spent the night in a shabby, run-down Days Inn of Fergus Falls, had breakfast at Perkins, then paid our $2 at the Otter Tail County Historical Museum, which got us into the E.T. Barnard Library. Two young people were there to assist. I got two folders full of Cole clippings. There were a lot of Coles in the county, many of them from New York, but with names completely unfamiliar. I ended up printing obits from the microfilm reader, finding all but Levi Cole's. I also copied part of Sarah's memoir with Tillie's reminiscences interspersed.

Tillie's imprint was apparent at the Otter Tail County Museum. She was active while living in Pelican Rapids and kept up correspondence with the historical society after her move to Denver. Her letters are detailed, much like her sister Georgina's letters. In an April 10, 1950, letter to Mr. E.T. Barnard at the Otter Tail County Historical Society, she is unsure if she'll be able to attend the society's summer meeting at Otter Tail Lake. She goes on:

*Perhaps you will remember that I wrote you I didn't expect to return to Pelican at all last summer, but I did go, later, rather unexpectedly. So it goes. You see, I do not drive nor own a car, and am a poor traveler by R.R., so whatever trips I make are often unplanned, and I go 'At the drop of the hat,' so to speak.*

At the end of the letter, she then lists the people who attended the funeral of one of the daughters of a former butcher from Pelican. Her obsession with details affected her domestic life. In 1944 when my mother rented a room from Aunt Tillie in Denver while my father was stationed at nearby Camp Carson, my mother gave birth to their first child. Later, when my parents were ready to move back to Michigan, Aunt Tillie presented her niece with some additional charges: the cost of duplicating a key and 75¢ for a lid to cover a diaper pail. My mother had purchased a diaper pail but had no lid. Her aunt happened to have an extra metal cover that just fit. In spite of her penny-pinching, Aunt Tillie was affectionate and caring toward her niece.

We left Fergus and drove to Superior, Wisconsin, passing Brainerd, Minnesota, with its Paul Bunyan statue. I remembered it from childhood trips, on my way to Black Duck to visit my mother's Cocking relatives. On the way, we sailed over Duluth, faster in our Toyota than in any prairie schooner as we crossed the city's many bridges. Duluth managed to be industrial and cosmopolitan at the same time. That night we were out of Minnesota, back in Wisconsin, settled in at the Stockade Motel with a view of the bay. We moved with ease and speed across state borders, something the Coles had never experienced.

# LIVING IN THE WAGONS

## *Summer 1871*

*We had many hindrances before we could build any houses. After the trip to Alexandria, some of our horses got homesick and started back to Wisconsin but were overtaken and brought back. During that first summer we had a terrific wind-storm and deluge of rain in the night, tearing down some of the largest trees. One large maple beside our wagon went down, but luckily did not fall across it, or we would probably have been killed; and a very large basswood fell toward us, but just far enough away so the tips of the top branches brushed down our milk-rack, which was made by nailing two ironwood poles each side of two medium-sized trees at the right height from the ground, and by covering each pan with another, it answered our purpose very well. That was an experience, but we only felt thankful that not one of us was hurt.*

—Sarah Moore Leonard Cole

arah's recounting of her first summer in Minnesota achieved its stiff-upper-lip tone because it was told forty-four years later. Many horrific and disheartening events become challenging, affirming adventures in hindsight. Most of the above entry, the part about the storm, was omitted from the text published in 1915 in the *St. Paul Farmers' Dispatch*. I finally got a copy of the 1915 newspaper account by calling the Minnesota Historical Society. My hours at the microfilm reader during my visit to St. Paul had been frustrating, but a more experienced reader of old newspapers at the society found the article and sent it to me. Using a magnifying glass, I read the edited, flat story.

Was she upset at the way her details and descriptions were cut? I'm fortunate to have her uncut version, for therein lies the poetry of her life and journey. Therein lay the details that captured my attention and drew me to my great-grandmother.

Having had some tense exchanges with newspaper editors over changes in my text—and style—I'm upset for her. The editor's hatchet is there, omitting lines and paragraphs and changing words to present a less passionate Sarah. When Sarah says they "were all fired up" with their plans, it is changed to "were afire." When she says they had "Minnesota fever hard," the newspaper prints it "Minnesota fever right." Sarah writes that she "could not see the stars only as the wind swayed the tree-tops." The newspaper changes it to "I could see the stars now and then as the wind swayed the tree-tops."

If the account in the *Farmers' Dispatch* had been my only source, I would have never known those details that made me want to take the journey, those details that gave me a feel for daily life in the 1870s. The newspaper leaves out Sarah's inventory of the wagon's contents; the mention of fruit trees grown from seed in the Coles' Wisconsin orchard; the fact that one of the Cole men rode a Kanuck pony on the journey. I would never have known that she "chafed in mind" because they weren't able to spend time in the city of St. Paul; that a daughter of William Henry nearly drowned in the Pomme de Terre River; that their baby's first birthday was the day they arrived in Pelican Rapids.

Like the name of the river they crossed, which would provide me with a signpost in following her trail, the name Prairie Lake was also omitted from the newspaper account. These place names are like diamonds when doing research. Just the words *Pomme de Terre* fall off the lips and onto the ear as testimony to the unknown, the foreign, the exotic just under the surface of the familiar. They are witness to the French fur traders who traveled the ruts of the Red River Trail. And *Prairie Lake*—it's like a whisper of stories told by my mother and aunts, stories I never paid much attention to while growing up. But as a grown-up, *Pomme de Terre River* and *Prairie Lake* took on magical qualities.

Perhaps the editor of the newspaper saw less value in the domestic details that Sarah included: the chicken coops torn off the sides of the wagon as they "carved a roadway to [their] claims," and the chickens and ducks following the wagons; the baking of biscuits in the portable tin oven; the forty-some mile trip to Alexandria on horseback to take out homestead papers. These chores of pioneering give texture to my family history. In the rather over-blown, flowery prose of journalism at that time, it's curious that these homey, yet essential, parts of Sarah's experience were omitted.

*On one claim was a small shack and a little start for clearing, and this the father took, so they had an 'excuse' for a house. We and the brother's family lived in our wagons all summer, and the three families were not forty rods from one another. The men planted potatoes about the middle of June, and in six weeks we began to eat young potatoes from our own garden. I never saw such potatoes as they were when matured; one could carry them on the arm like stove wood. The men also cleared a piece on a hill that had not much but brush and peavines on it, and sowed some buckwheat, but that did not amount to much. Then the horses and cows must have hay for the winter. There was plenty along the river for the taking, and that was the next thing in order, though this was difficult on account of the gnats and flies which were almost insufferable.*

*That first summer the grass-hopper pest arrived, and my sister-in-law and myself spent hours with long-stemmed brushes going up and down among the potatoes driving the hoppers away, and we saved them too, but the hoppers came back for several years, and were a great damage to grain crops on the prairie. We were glad we had chosen the woods, for we could have a winter crop when the sawmill was built, and our timber had a ready market. There was no need to run in debt for farm machinery and implements. We traded our horses for oxen, as they were more suitable for our use and less expense to keep; besides the difference in price gave us something to help our expenses. Our flour came from Sauk Center [sic], 110 miles away, but I can truly say we never felt the lack of any needful thing to eat, or drink, or wear.*

The newspaper piece doesn't mention the closeness of the three families that summer. I'd love to know how the family dynamics changed. How did Sarah get on with her mother-in-law and her sister-in-law now that they'd reached Minnesota? If there were tensions, they were eased when each family had its own house. The *Farmers' Dispatch* printed "father," rather than "the father"; and "my brother," instead of "the brother." Here the newspaper completely

91

misinforms as to the familial relationships. During the summer of 1871, Sarah was the only Leonard among all Coles.

Even though the potatoes weren't ready until August, finding food was not a huge problem. They might have bartered or traded for staples. They had the butter churn, the tin oven, cows for milk, and the river and lake for fish. The woods had deer, bear, and smaller animals.

Sarah and Mary Elizabeth, her sister-in-law, battled the grasshoppers, according to Sarah's account, during their first summer in Minnesota, the summer of 1871. Historical texts limit the great grasshopper, or more correctly "Rocky Mountain locust," invasion to 1873–1877. Those most devastated by the swarms were farmers who grew wheat, oats, corn, and barley. Grasshopper plagues were not new in the 1870s. In 1767, an explorer of the territory that would one day be called Minnesota commented that locusts arrived every seven years and infested "these parts ... in large swarms, and [did] a great deal of mischief."[24]

In 1871, new families and businesses were encouraged to prosper. There was plenty of space; development spelled progress. The goal was to bring modern facilities to within reach of the pioneers. They didn't travel by wagon to get away from it all, but to spread progress across the continent. Commentary in an 1882 issue of the *Fergus Falls Journal* reiterates this idea:

> *H. Harris is platting off his farm into town lots, as lots sell from $25 to $500 each. It is a pleasure to see these old settlers turn their wheat fields into corner lots and their plow shares into pleasure carriages. Others with large interests are Mr. Blyberg, Geo. B. Wright and R.L. Frazee.*[25]

## Summer 1998, post-Pelican, back in Michigan

In July Norm and I bought ten acres with lots of red pine, many of them in rows, an old orchard, and lots of blackberry brambles. Perhaps a tree farm was the plan by a former owner. I know more about the old farms of Pelican Rapids, Minnesota, than I do about the one where we'll build a house. It seems a shame to ruin it with a building, though. I'm experiencing builder's guilt. Once the well-drilling equipment and the heavy trucks and bulldozers come roaring in, things will never be the same. We've already startled grouse, snakes, rabbits. We haven't seen deer yet, but the heart-shaped tracks are everywhere. The people who live up the road had their birdfeeder demolished by a bear.

The land heaves and bucks, creating little hills and dales. One ridge, which we've named Fern Hill, is covered with waist-high ferns. That's where I want to look as I stand before the kitchen sink. We take picnics to the site and eat near a spreading juniper shrub, a local growth. We vow to save this one when the excavation begins. We've been outlining the footprint of the house, using stakes and twine. There are trees in every room. We've piled rocks where the woodstove and chimney will stand, within the center square, the core, the heart of the house. Norm's design is influenced by the floor plan of a house on Beaver Island, where we stayed one weekend. It will be a flowing house with lots of light. Norm will also incorporate some Frank Lloyd Wright touches.

### August 1, 1998

*August—my month. I nearly cried yesterday, so happy was I to own land and to be standing on it, raking pine chippings on a path, gazing up at banks of ferns and a row of apple trees, studded with little reddening apples. I imagine applesauce, apple pies, cider—annual rituals with friends and neighbors.*

I wonder if this is the fun part—imagining, anticipating in this peaceful spot. The rise where our house will sit looks over acres of woods where trails climb, curve and fall. In the winter these are used for cross-country skiing. For this summer it's our spot; no one else comes out. That will end in September, when groundbreaking is scheduled. I find myself envying Sarah as she saw her new house go up. The relatives got together, along with their expert from New Brunswick, and they put up a house. We've talked about renting a trailer and living on the land as the house goes up. It would be similar to living in a wagon all summer. But we are burdened by so much stuff from our former lives, we've found it simpler to rent a house in town.

As the Coles experienced a land grab, so are we here in northern Michigan. The grabbiness is not for establishing farms, but capitalizing on the resort trade. Few farms remain. I take some comfort that our ten acres can never be subdivided and that we're surrounded by conservancy easement. Still our ten acres was once a part of someone's orchard or farm. I've always wanted to own land as a place of retreat, not necessarily to build on. When we drive out at the end of the day and carry a bottle of wine, some fruit, cheese, and crackers to the top of the slope where the house will sit, I try not to think of what it will mean to actually build here. My ambivalent feelings about building a new house come out in an early-morning journal entry:

> How can I tell you? I want you to leave the fifty red pine growing in our living room. And the sandy burrows under your study floor; leave them. The blackberry brambles, grabbing at our jeans' legs as we outline the driveway. Don't hack them. What will the birds and bears do, their wild mouths yearning for the sweet juice of August? Leave the chainsaw in the truck, let its horrible teeth be still. When I swung the scythe and cut down the bodies of ferns to make a path to the trail, I was sick for days. The scar in the long bank of green was a reproach. Startled birds had flown up, a disaster uprooting them from their comfortable home. Let's leave this land alone; we can find a nest easily enough. There are so few places anymore where they can live their natural lives without being evicted by greedy landlords.
>
> You see studs, beams, joists. You see a drawing materializing. I see St. Johnswort, clouds of purple knapweed, wild pea.

I don't know, but I doubt if Sarah had these feelings of disturbing the land. Although her words express an awareness and knowledge of nature, there is no reverence, nor awe. Nature just is. It's a presence that needs to be dealt with in order to live a civilized life. As I've grown older, I've become more needy of being in contact with natural surroundings. I ache for hills, water, trees. This ache brought me to northern Michigan. I get my connections, my feeling of being a part of things by spending time in the woods or on a lake. I have a voracious hunger for knowing the names of everything—ground cover with lacy needles; gray-green lichen with red tips; the flock of birds in the maple that I've only seen once; the small, soft, caramel-colored pelt in the middle of the trail—what delicate little animal had its head chewed off?

Unlike Sarah with her huge potatoes and unlucky buckwheat, it will be awhile before we plant a garden. Anything we put in the ground will be at the mercy of rabbits, deer, porcupines (or whatever constructs those deep,

ankle-breaking holes in the ground). We'll have to learn all kinds of strate-
gies for growing vegetables and flowers. I want to start a compost pile, but it
could attract the black bears.

We don't have a river close by. Lake Michigan is five miles away. However,
there is a swampy area down among the trails, with lovely clear pools, car-
peted brown with leaves on the bottom. We, too, have the insects to contend
with. We've been bitten by blackflies during the day and by mosquitoes in
the early summer mornings and evenings. So far, there has been no plague
of grasshoppers.

# BUILDING THE HOUSE

## Early fall 1871

*Then came house building, first for the older brother, as he had quite a large family, two girls and three boys, and a very commodius [sic] log cabin was soon in process of building. After that came ours, which we moved into in October, and if it had been a palace we could not have felt prouder of it. We fell in with a man from New Brunswick, who had a claim near us, an old lumberman, and what he could do with a 'broad-axe' was surprising. There was no lumber to be had as yet, (although the good water-power at the village brought about a sawmill and other facilities very soon), but he hewed the basswood trees into boards for window-casings, doors and table tops, hewed one side of logs for 'puncheon' floor, and matched them so it was a very good, solid floor. None of the other settlers had any kind of floor except hay, while we could boast of a parlor in one end of our cabin, with a new rag carpet, and kitchen in the other end with a beautiful white floor. Our roofs were covered with poles resting on a log that reached across the top of the walls from end to end, the poles being covered with hay, then earth on top of that.*

*In lieu of chairs we had stools made of a basswood log split and one side hewn smooth, with logs in augur holes on the rounded side beneath, and the many kinds of conveniences we could manufacture in this primitive way were a great satisfaction, though our table was very wobbly after the legs had shrunk; however it was a table, and strongly made.*

—Sarah Moore Leonard Cole

B uilding a house in western Minnesota, still the frontier, was not as easy as construction in the more settled Lemonweir Valley. In their new location, everything had to be done from scratch. Since most of the

Coles' possessions had been sold when they left Wisconsin, all the furniture had to be built.

The house building for William Henry's family took precedence. William and Mary had five children already (there would be three more born in Minnesota), so their cabin needed to be "commodious." Most likely the girls (Hannah Lucetta and Margaret Elizabeth) had their own bedroom, as did the boys (Karl Frederick, William Henry II, and Samuel Edward).

The newspaper version of Sarah's story changed the phrase "fell in with" to "formed a friendship." Falling in with a man from New Brunswick has a much riskier, slightly shady tone. But this lumberman from New Brunswick turned out to be a lucky find. It's no wonder that Sarah found his use of the broadaxe "surprising" because basswood is soft, close-grained, and hard to split. Also known as the American linden, its uses ran from carriage bodies to shoe soles. After the fragrant white blossoms in late spring, the basswoods put out generous foliage to provide dense shade for humans and cattle during the sweltering summer. The Coles were among the pioneers who cut down the virgin forests of lindens. Nature was there to provide for them and to be conquered. They were still part of the "wooden age" in America. All their needs came from the forest.

Although more sophisticated types of roofing were being used, the Minnesota pioneers kept it simple, going to the woods and fields for roofing materials. The metal roofs in more settled areas, like the corrugated, galvanized roofs of the California Gold Rush houses, were not available. At the same time the Coles were moving into their house, the Chicago Fire destroyed 17,450 buildings,[26] including Samuel Barrett's plant which produced "fireproof" composition roofing.[27] From Sarah's account, it seems that her and George's cabin was covered with a sod roof. Although the roof was primitive, the smooth puncheon floor in the parlor was covered with the thirty-five yards of rag carpeting brought from Wisconsin.

## Late summer through remainder of 1998
### August 19

*Drove 3 hrs. to Bay City to Baywood Truss. Signed and paid for an engineering plan. They will put up shell 'around' Oct. 15. First we need their foundation plan for Sackrider who will do foundation, well, septic—starting 'around' Sept. 15. And a roofing guy has been lined up—we'll go with metal (steel). Now for the fascia and soffit—wood or aluminum? We'll live in a rented house, not our wagon, while all this transpires.*

**August 24**

*Mild-mannered guy from Top of Michigan came out for line from utility pole to house for temporary set-up. Norm has expended buckets of sweat clearing a 7 ft. wide path for the 181 feet.*

**Sept. 1**

*Well permit $185; building permit around $650. We've got at least two weeks before groundbreaking. Went out last night for a walk with the dogs and a glass of wine on the 'deck.' No work—just a peaceful, easy feeling. It becomes more interesting and beautiful every time we go out. The apple trees are groaning with fruit. The twine and stakes have been disturbed by the locals (animals).*

*Sept. 11*

*Have not worked on property all week. Last Sunday we picked apples with Sharon and Jim—at least 5 varieties. Next week groundbreaking!*

**Sept. 17**

*The hole exists. Septic tank put in. Sunk before I saw it. Bulldozer, chipper, trucks, and biggest backhoe in the world! Norm on site all day. Woke up with bad headache during night.*

**Sept. 18**

*Pipes being laid in drain field … About twenty minutes to 5 the big cement truck for laying the footers arrived.*

**Sept. 22**

*While out at the site on Sunday, Jim and Norm noticed a big hole in the septic tank. 'Green cement' was Jim's diagnosis. We're getting a new one. The block (10") goes up on Thursday.*

### Sept. 25

*The first course of block was laid yesterday, but the crew didn't show up today. They 'thought it might rain.' It was slightly overcast but a beautiful balmy day. With 13 courses in the foundation, it's only just begun.*

*Faxed plans have been piling up from Bay City. Every tiny change is looked at, then Norm calls them back. We experience moments of frustration with them, and I'm sure vice versa. Tonight at 4:45 we saw they'd left out the wall where the floor to ceiling bookcases will go.*

### Sept. 30

*Rain began at noon. Went out to lot at 5 with dogs. New basement floor was flooded. Corners were built up, but cement between blocks was squishy. Depressing. I sloshed around picking up debris—wrappers, McDonald's cups, cans—left by workers.*

### Oct. 9

*Foundation completed! Looks big, bigger than footprint of house when outlined in stakes & twine. Chimney bricks arrived from G.R.*

### Oct. 15

*Our house arrived! Piles of white lumber beside the foundation.*

### Oct. 16

*As wind whipped up, Norm and I struggled and cursed to secure plastic and huge tarps over lumber.*

### Oct. 31

*House wrapped in Tyvek by Dupont. Its lines revealed. We view it from all angles on the trail below.*

★　★　★

By the end of October, Sarah, George, and baby Georgina were in their new house preparing for a Minnesota winter. What kind of a winter was it? We're living on borrowed time. No snow yet. I remember previous years when the snow arrived by Halloween. But this fall of 1998 is a time of grace—and a time of trash.

With each new step in the building, another pile of disposed goods appears. I spend weekends picking up after the workmen: McDonald's containers, pop cans, bottles, Styrofoam coffee cups only half-finished. I've picked up nails and staples by the hundreds on the ground around the house. Strips of cellophane and plastic wrapping are caught in the low branches of the red pine and are snagged by blackberry bushes. A carpet of cigarette butts litters the inside and outside of the new structure. Putting trash cans in the house doesn't seem to help.

Trees, hay, earth. Sarah had no piles of leftover laminated scraps from door and window frames; no clumps of pink insulation; no strips of OSB; no slivers of metal and hundreds of screws, staples, and nails. The old lumberman from New Brunswick, who Sarah and George "fell in with," created few leftovers with his broadaxe.

When the foundation was laid, we noticed tar buckets, cans, and bottles in the earth beside the cement block courses. A friend told us it's common for excavators to backfill over the construction trash. We cleaned up around the foundation. The thought of erecting a new home on top of trash was unsettling. It seemed like a desecration.

## Nov. 4

*Well drilling and metal roof start today. Windows and cedar siding have not arrived. Mason says chimney will be completed by Friday. We ordered the woodstoves on Monday.*

## Nov. 25

*Roof 90% completed. Some pieces still missing. Most windows in. Everything has slowed down during deer season. However, ceramic tile is in for center square. Norm rented a propane heater to keep the cement/grout from freezing at night. Tues. he was out there at 4 a.m. to check. This morning (his birthday) he went out at 6 a.m. to turn it off; it was out of fuel anyway. Next week—plumbing and heating. Melie was here for two weeks. Most of [rough] wiring is done.*

## Dec. 3

*After numerous delays, siding was delivered yesterday. Baywooders arrived today. Tuesday we went to Cheboygan to order another woodstove that will work with our flues and opening. A soapstone stove should be in Dec. 8. 50s today. How much longer can this last? New reserve tank (WellTrol) on pump looks better than the fiberglass one. Two surly guys replaced it.*

## Dec. 18

*Yesterday the Baywood crew 'buttoned it up.' Front door, garage doors and basement windows finally in. Still unfinished roofing. Parts aren't in. Meanwhile water is soaking the plywood under the roof in the garage. Unresolved problems with windows. The triangular ones upstairs don't fit properly, and the real oak we expected is simply a thin 'printed' layer over pine. As of now, the window company will put in oak sills on the downstairs windows.*

*All problems are now covered by snow. It snowed yesterday and has been all today. It seems more normal for northern Michigan. The ski people are relieved.*

*Yesterday the plumbers had trouble getting up Stutsmanville. We didn't go out today. Both of us felt ill. I wonder if anyone got in today. We need to get someone to plow the driveway. Yesterday Norm presented me with a key to our new home.*

# SETTLING IN

## *1872, 1873*

*In February following our emigration we had a son added to our family, and when he was about a year old I was engaged to teach the first school we had. It was held in a log shanty about three-quarters of a mile from our home, in the direction of the village. The brother's wife offered to take my baby as I passed her house on my way to school, and I picked him up on my return. They had four children of school age then and were very anxious to have me teach them and others. There was quite a number from the village, perhaps 20 in all. My little girl went with me to school, and learned much, though nothing was required of her except to be quiet. As I went through the woods in the autumn, carrying the baby, I would scuff my feet among the dry leaves to see him laugh at the rustling noise. After leaving him I would catch the three-year-old girl up on my back to hurry along, for time was precious, as I had no help, and did all the housework we had done. But I was well and had no end of life and ambition to help things along, and enjoyed the teaching, which I kept up for several terms, having some help about housework after the first term.*

*I taught the first four terms in the village of Pelican Rapids, and two or three in the district northeast of us later, walking from home with my two children and those of the brother-in-law, through the woods, a distance of a mile and a half. We often came upon bears' tracks, and there were also deer, rabbits, partridges and other game in those woods.*

—Sarah Moore Leonard Cole

The son born in 1872 was my great-uncle, Evander Leonard Cole, known as "Bud" to his family. My mother has always referred to him

103

as Uncle Van; he died before she was born but achieved legendary status to my mother's generation of Coles.

Like his mother, Evander began his working life as a country school teacher; however, at twenty-one, he decided to change paths and became the cashier in the Pelican Rapids bank. Craving an even bigger change, in 1898 at the age of twenty-six, he and his friend Will Harris set out for the Klondike. Their grueling adventure did not end with finding gold, and the two young men returned to Pelican, Will Harris walking with a strange gait due to the loss of most of his toes. Evander had been forced to cut gangrenous material from his companion's feet when they became frostbitten. Evander wrote an account of this harrowing adventure, "The Deadly Edmonton Trail," which was published in the *Alaska Sportsman* in 1955, long after his death. Will Harris married Evander's older sister Georgina in 1916.

A few years after the Klondike expedition, Evander moved to Scottville, Michigan, where he managed the State Savings Bank of Scottville, owned by C.W. McPhail. (His son, Larry MacPhail, became the general manager of the Brooklyn Dodgers in the 1930s.) In 1904 Evander married Kathryn Quirk, a woman with family wealth, who was a Catholic. He immersed himself in civic life, becoming a tireless dynamo in the small town's organizations. In 1907 he became Scottville's first mayor.

Although neither Georgina nor Tillie attended college, Evander was determined to get a college education for the youngest and other son, Daniel, my grandfather. Evander sent a rather stern, lay-it-on-the-line letter, penned on The State Savings Bank of Scottville stationery, to his mother.

*June 1st, 1906*

*Dear Mother:*

*Yours and father's letters received and though I haven't time to write a real letter I have a word to say regarding Dan that I want to get said.*

*He has talent in several directions and should receive the best kind of an education. Such an education he can get. There isn't a better place to secure such an education than at the University of Michigan at Ann Arbor. This "U" ranks as one of the best in the country and a young man can fit himself for anything from Mining Engineer to Preacher.*

Here is my proposition to him and to you: If he will come to me with High School certificates showing him a graduate with fair honors from the P.R. High School, and if he will bring with him $50.00 that he has earned himself and $100.00 given him by you and father, if he will agree to report to me once a month his progress, his expenses necessary or unnecessary and will bind himself to stay by the deal as long as I will stay by him I will go with him right to Ann Arbor and see to his matriculation and help him select a boarding place and he never need quit (and he must bind himself not to quit) until he graduates.

He may never have as good a proposition made him and certainly you never will get a chance to educate him well on $100.00 again.

I want you to put that much in the deal so you will have an interest in the matter that will make him feel responsible to you for good use of the privilege of such an education and I want him to earn part -$50.00 to start with and I shall expect him to do as thousands of the students do, is work some outside school hours to defray board etc. as opportunity shows up. Thousands earn their whole way in this way, and many are the places offered students to do this kind of work to defray room rent etc.

Even with him doing this and with hard work with his books so as to make the course as short as possible it cannot but take from $1000. to $1500. in money from me to put him through.

I shall want to own him from the day he comes to me until he shows me his sheepskin, and shall expect to have full right to jack him up if reports show needless waste of money or time, shall expect to make a trip there once in awhile to find out what sort of company he keeps etc. In short if he wants an education bad enough to enlist under me he can have it, but I won't stand for foolishness.

Now don't persuade him but if he wants to accept this offer I am ready to stand to it.

Lovingly your son,
E. L. Cole

The letter is directed to Sarah, not George. Perhaps Evander avoided dealing with his father because of the difficulty they had getting along. Evander sounds more like the parent as he lays down the ground rules. Dan was seventeen in 1906 and did not accept this offer from his older brother, but by

1910 he had graduated from Ferris Institute. It isn't clear if Evander helped fund his courses. Dan followed his older brother into banking, taking a position in Walkerville, Michigan, where he worked in a branch of the State Savings Bank of Scottville.

Evander, named after Sarah's father, was killed in a deer-hunting accident by a young guide near Munising in Michigan's Upper Peninsula in 1919. This baby, who laughed at the noise his mother made as she kicked up the autumn leaves while carrying him through the Minnesota woods, died when he was 47, before both his parents. Just before his death, he had built Sarah and George a bungalow in Scottville. The elder Coles sold their home in Pelican Rapids and moved, but they were back in Minnesota within a few months. There are family stories of Evander's explosive temper and friction between George and Evander. My aunt remembers hearing of Uncle Van pushing someone through the window at the bank and of jerking a phone out of the wall. The clash of personalities must have made his death doubly upsetting. Sarah and George, having barely returned to Pelican when Evander was killed, perhaps with hard feelings on both sides, did not make the journey back to Michigan for Bud's funeral.

Evander's death notice in the local Michigan newspaper referred to his death as a loss, not only to the town of Scottville, but to all of Mason County. "It is irreparable. No one can take his place in public admiration. Like most brave men he made light of all hardships met in the path of duty." The long, flowery obituary included comment on his strong devotion to education.

> Mr. Cole's last public utterances were given at the Teachers' Institute at Community hall the evening before his departure on this fateful hunting trip when he took time from his hurry of preparation to give a talk upon 'The School as an Investment' urging school patrons to deal less in a destructive criticism and give more of constructive suggestion.

Another tribute accentuates his position in the community: "When the news flashed over the wire that E.L. Cole was dead, it seemed that the very pulse of Scottville had ceased to beat." The piece ends: "Turn down the light. Evander L. Cole lived not in vain." He wielded his forceful personality in all areas of his life. His public persona may have been more admired than his private one.

★   ★   ★

In 1872 Sarah was a mother with a baby and a toddler. In her way, she was balancing career and motherhood, without many of the complexities faced by today's mothers of young children. She went to work as a teacher, with the assurance of quality childcare for her baby. And she was able to bring her little girl to the job. William Henry and Mary Elizabeth's children benefited by having a teacher they could trust. I doubt if Sarah had discipline problems in the classroom. Children being taught by their aunt who was also their neighbor were probably on their best behavior.

*A Century at the Rapids* records that Pelican's first schoolhouse was "a log structure located a short distance west of the Putnam bridge," and that Mrs. George W. Cole was the first teacher. The children included four of Sarah's nieces and nephew, six others, plus Georgina and Bud.

> *The children sat in slab seats without backs or desks, except Bud, who lay in a hammock suspended from the ceiling just back of his mother's desk. When Bud awoke hungry, school was dismissed for recess, after he was fed and quieted, school was called and study resumed.*[28]

When I think of recent battles by young mothers to be allowed to nurse at the workplace, I'm impressed with Sarah's handling of the situation and with the way education and domestic life were not segregated. Sarah's motherhood and teaching were of a whole cloth.

## *Summer 1999*
## *July 5–8*

*Last March we saw paw prints in the snow (they were broad and big, distinctive compared to the heart-shaped deer tracks) at the bottom of the hill, where a path on our ten acres joins the main trail of conservancy easement acreage. We continued taking the same route for our late afternoon walks. We talked loudly, announcing our presence. We made the dogs stay on the path.*

107

*Near the middle of June we moved into our nearly completed house. Now our relationship with the bear was permanent. The bear here must feel much like the locals, those who have lived in northern Michigan for four or five generations. The building of another house, another golf course, cuts down on their habitat. All the 'free' places have become private. I do feel guilty, like an interloper in my new house.*

*Our summer walks are less carefree than in spring or fall. First Norm noticed a berry-laden bush, really a skinny tree, with a limb snapped off and claw marks high up on the main trunk. The next day bushes on both sides of the path were in shambles. No manners. We tasted the red berries. Kind of mushy with a hint of sweetness. These are serviceberries. Their white flowers are profuse in early spring. Their name comes from an association with funerals. Bodies could be buried in the thawed ground when the white flowers bloomed as a signal.*

*Then we saw a neat pile of dark shit, red-flecked with berry skins right at the start of a new path Norm had cleared. Is this communication, or what? Now we've been taking other routes for our walks. When we do take the 'bear path' down at the bottom of the hill, we talk loudly and Norm bangs together two pieces of chrome bar.*

I see many of the same animal tracks that Sarah observed as I hike through the woods that surround Second Growth, our name for the property. Seeing the bear tracks for the first time within sight of the house stopped my breathing as I bent to study the wide pad and defined claw marks in the sandy soil. The idea that wild animals are carrying on their lives within a quarter mile of my living room impresses me. I doubt if Sarah was too impressed by the wild things near their homestead. I'm sure she romanticized less about animals—she regarded them as an ordinary part of her surroundings. Most of her life was lived outside cities and towns, so she was not removed from the natural world. The possibility of finding a bear in the living room (or on the deck, as happened to the neighbors), a porcupine in the basement, a snake in the bathroom gives an edge to daily life. We're living on these acres by grace, not by manifest destiny. I feel grateful to be here, lucky even, but with reservations. Beneath these feelings lurks a shadowy suspicion that I may be doing more to upset the balance of things than hunters or snowmobilers, two groups who don't have access to conservancy land.

\*   \*   \*

In June we moved in, entranced by the reality of the blueprint. We both wandered through the house, looking at the views from every window. We can't yet experience the feeling of "settling in," for there are so many loose ends, hundreds of half-finished things, as well as discoveries about what needs to be done to get the approval of the host of house inspectors.

### August 3

*Aching, both of us, from yesterday's evening in the trench. The bulldozer will be back this morning to finish grading the front slope. Norm needed to run pipe about three feet down in the ground—PVC that would go from the garage drain in the side of the house, run under the LP pipe and divert water down the hill. We struggled connecting an elbow in the twilight, plagued by mosquitoes, covered with reddish soil that lies beneath the sandy surface. A great feeling of accomplishment when the connected pipe finally lay in its trench. The discomfort and frustration were worth it ... Two bucks and a doe at 6:50 a.m. walking from their orchard beds into the woods.*

Besides the trails and woods, Norm and I are drawn to the little township cemetery, a half-mile from our house. Since our trip to Pelican, I've changed my attitude toward cemeteries. I see them as places of peace and solace. The inhabitants of this graveyard are all from the nineteenth century. The township keeps it mowed, and on Memorial Day, the Civil War veterans get flags on their stones. It is a link with the Coles, for these people were contemporaries of Sarah and George and their children: Andrew Maples (father), 1840–1905; John Wesley Starr (father), 1835–1885; Delia Wilma Starr (daughter), 1874–1894. Several gravestones are arranged around a tall stone marker, engulfed by a lilac bush, for the Hoddinott family. Joseph (1842–1924) and Mina (1851–1910) lived on while some of their children died young: George (1882–1888) and Esther (1892–1899). Many of the dates are hard to read, so lichen-encrusted are the stones, all the indentations filled in with the grayish growth. Even sadder than the children's graves are the unmarked ones. A semi-circle of stone stands in the grass; further on, two narrow wooden tombstone-shaped markers measure off a four-foot length of earth. Who is buried here? There are no names or dates to spark the visitor into imagining their lives.

One night after returning from a walk to the cemetery, we phoned for a pizza. They didn't deliver this far out, so we had to drive into town. I ordered a mushroom, black olive, red pepper pizza, and gave the name *Sarah Cole*.

# INDIANS—A DISMAL TUNE

## *1870s—after New Ulm*

*We had the Indians, too, one or two families of them lived only a short distance up the lake from us, and they would drive anywhere through the woods with their home-made cart and pony, over logs and brush which might be in the way, and the wheels creaked a dismal tune. They were not hostile and did not bother us much by begging, for they did not like to make the acquaintance of our dog, and they never dare kill a dog. But we did have two genuine Indian scares; the first time we fled in haste, leaving our supper untouched on the table, as well as everything else. The women and children were gathered in one of the houses in the village, the men with weapons standing guard in and around the store. Of course we did not sleep much, but told Indian tales until we had a first-class scare. Meantime we engaged a friendly half-breed to scout around and find out if the report that the Indians intended a raid was true. He assured us that there was nothing to fear, that the Indians feared us more than we did them, so we returned to our homes in peace, and the next time we stayed at home and were unmolested.*

—Sarah Moore Leonard Cole

At the beginning of the 1860s, Minnesota had a large population of Sioux and Ojibwa. The 1862 uprising led by Little Crow resulted in the Sioux, as well as the Winnebago, being banished from Minnesota by an act of Congress. In what came to be known as the Sioux Uprising, which included the New Ulm Massacre, 737 men, women, and children were killed, with hundreds more taken as prisoners.[29] The resentment among the Sioux toward the federal government had been festering. Money and food had been promised in a previous treaty, but like many treaties, this one produced mostly empty promises. Starvation roamed the prairie.

The event was sparked when a small band of Santee Sioux killed five whites near New Ulm in mid-August. Panic infected the area as stories quickly spread of a fullscale Indian insurrection. Seeing the reaction of the settlers, the Sioux knew they must fight or flee. Some left Minnesota. However, Little Crow and thirteen hundred warriors stayed on their land and attacked settlements in the Minnesota River Valley. Finally Colonel Henry Sibley led local militia in overcoming the Sioux. Many fled to the Dakotas, and even on to Canada, taking white hostages with them.

Within a few months of the last battle (the Battle of Wood Lake), 303 Sioux were brought to trial for their part in the rebellion. They were sentenced to death by hanging; however, President Lincoln intervened and the number of condemned was brought down to thirty-eight. The largest mass execution in the United States took place at Mankato on Dec. 26, 1862— thirty-eight men climbed onto a large platform and had nooses placed around their necks. The condemned Sioux were all hung at the same time.[30]

Otter Tail County, which would later include Pelican Rapids, was emptied of settlers after the uprising. But shortly after the four Minnesota Sioux tribes, along with some Winnebago, were expelled from their land, prairie schooners were again rolling across western Minnesota. Land once used freely by the natives was considered "unoccupied public land" by the government. The Homestead Act, which had become official on May 20, 1862, allowed settlers to claim up to 160 acres.

Sarah's father probably had the Sioux in mind when he warned the young couple about Indians in Minnesota. The native people that Sarah encountered were most likely Ojibwa. They were not ousted in 1863 and about six thousand lived on various reservations in the northern forests. Because of white settler nervousness in the aftermath of New Ulm, a treaty was implemented to concentrate the peaceful Ojibwa on one large tract. They ceded to the U.S. government Gull Lake, Mille Lacs, Sandy Lake, Rabbit Lake, Rice Lake, and Pokegama Lake reservations in exchange for a large section near Leech Lake.[31] The U.S. government did not let up on its infringement on the Ojibwa way of life. In the 1880s, more than forty thousand acres of rice fields were flooded when the U.S. Army Corps of Engineers built dams on the reservation. The Ojibwa were further aggrieved when the government's payment was totally insufficient for the damage.[32]

Back in Wisconsin, the Coles had lived with the Winnebago, who were often regarded as "non-treaty abiding."[33] There had been attempts in the past to relocate them in the west, but they worked their way back to Juneau County. They regarded Wisconsin as their homeland and believed they had legal title to the land. They would not go away. Chief Lemonweir told of wearing out six pair of moccasins walking back to Juneau County from Nebraska in the 1870s. They would not stay on reservations, and finally the federal government recognized their right to homestead in Wisconsin. Under the Indian Homestead Act, they were exempt from property taxes.[34]

The Coles' homestead in Minnesota was on Ojibwa land. In 1869 the Ojibwa offered land near Prairie Lake to a Swedish settler. The settler was only too glad to claim about a hundred acres of natural clearing. The native people believed the area to be haunted by the spirits of ancestors who had died in battle. One possible explanation for the "haunting" was fox fire, bio-luminescence caused by certain fungi growing in decaying wood. Some have hypothesized that flares of marsh gas caused the mysterious glow. The Swede built his first home, a dugout into the side of a hill, then planted wheat.[35]

In the 1870s and '80s, the Indians were considered part of the natural setting, like the bear and deer. It was not uncommon to see Indians in their canoes on Prairie Lake and the Pelican River. The whites sometimes regarded them as a nuisance or concern, but not really dangerous. Although Sarah knew which families were French and which were German, the native people were referred to as "Indians," without any tribal association. In 1915, when Sarah's account was printed in the *Farmers' Dispatch*, the editor changed "one or two families of them" to "one or two families of 'Reds.'"

The attitude toward the Native Americans by the white settlers reminds me of the Irish disposition toward the tinkers (also referred to as "travellers" or "gypsies") in the environs of Dublin. While on a visit there, I was warned that they stole and begged, so I should avoid them—not even make eye contact. They were considered an interesting footnote to the culture, but a disreputable one.

When Sarah mentions that "they never dare kill a dog," was she referring to a respect, or fear, the natives had for dogs— or was she implying that they would never try to kill an animal belonging to a white? The native people were not part of the plan for a progressive world; they were accepted to some extent, but not valued.

What would the Coles have thought of today's Native Americans in Minnesota and Wisconsin, who have reasserted some claims to the land they hunted, fished, and lived on? There have been a few cases of old treaties being honored. Today there are around two hundred thousand Ojibwa, with around eighteen tribal organizations recognized by the federal government.[36]

# BECOMING A LOCAL

## 1875

*I think it was in 1875 that my husband decided to spend the winter work-*
*ing in the woods on Height-of-the-Land Lake, and I engaged to teach a*
*school near a neighboring town, Elizabeth, Minn., about twelve miles from*
*home, in a German neighborhood. I took our two children (the girl five,*
*the boy three) and bed and provision, and was allowed a room and many*
*kindnesses in the home of a French family near the school house. That was*
*the most interesting school I ever had charge of; about 40 pupils, and many*
*of them nearly grown young men and women. The parents were as much*
*interested as we, and stood loyally by me in my work and discipline. The*
*Germans being musical, I taught them to read notes and many songs. This*
*we enjoyed, and we entertained the parents at spelling-bees and whenever*
*they visited us, with part-songs, rounds, etc. I had to take my children with*
*me, but they were great favorites and gave no trouble. That term lasted four*
*months, and I was persuaded to teach the summer term of three months, my*
*husband staying with his parents, who had cared for our stock during the*
*winter. So we cleaned up quite a little cash, which was scarce in those days.*
*My wages were $40 a month, and I was offered $50 to return the following*
*winter, but we felt we could not bear to have our home broken up any longer.*
*That was not my last term of school, but I did not leave home again.*

"I did not leave home again." The situation of George and Sarah living and
working apart defies the stereotype of the "traditional" family. Their separation was driven by economics, as were most of the major upheavals and
geographic changes in the Cole family. Sarah's job, only twelve miles away
from the house, required a relocation. It is indicative of the close bond she

had with her young children that Sarah took them with her to live in a room, rather than leave them with her in-laws.

The raw prairie settlement quickly organized for social events. According to newspaper reports, the Fourth of July in 1871 was celebrated as a crowd of sixty sang "The Star Spangled Banner," listened to speeches, and held a dance. Sarah would have welcomed such a social event, after living in a wagon for several months out near Prairie Lake. In 1915 she recalled the entertainment offerings in the Pelican area.

> More settlers came. Soon there was a store, and we confidently looked forward to a thriving village. It has been slow in developing, but it is here now.
>
> We had really cultured people to mingle with and the good times of those early days will always be a pleasant memory. The first Sunday School was organized about 1873, and we had preaching. We always celebrated the Fourth of July in good style, and with a dancing party occasionally. Once we went nine miles to a leap year dance. My sister-in-law furnished one ox and I the other for our team, and we rode out across the prairie to the place where the dance was held. Of course, it was no end of fun, as we had a jolly load.

Sarah never had to worry about fitting into an established community, because she helped found it. There were not levels of seniority, not much opportunity for snobbery from the "older families." Undoubtedly this "older family" attitude developed as the area grew. But one appeal of prairie life had to have been its lack of entrenched social register, its "first come, first served" approach.

For the men, the Freemasons gave them a sense of community in their new homes. The motto of the organization, "order out of chaos," seems to fit the settlers' zeal for taming the prairies, planning towns, and getting rid of all things foreign and not understood.

George Washington Cole was a Mason for over forty years. His obituary in the Pelican Rapids newspaper gives a clue to his precarious financial circumstance:

> [He took] his first three degrees in the Cornerstone Lodge, No. 99, of Fergus Falls, afterwards affiliating at Pelican Rapids when a lodge was started here. During the

*last few years, his funds running low, and not wishing to incur indebtedness, he*
*obtained his dimit from this lodge.*

His "dimit," or "dismissal" in Masonic vocabulary, meant that he resigned
and gave up his membership in the lodge. The obituary implies that he went
beyond the master's level in the lodge. (The third degree is master.) Leaving the organization cannot have been a decision that was made easily. Sons
Evander and Daniel became Masons, too. According to one aunt, Evander
dropped his association after he married a Catholic woman. (The Catholic Church has always taken a strong anti-Mason stance.) Dan joined the
Masons and went to Hart, a larger town than Walkerville, where he lived,
for his Masonic meetings. Dan's wife, Grace, heartily disapproved of these
gatherings.

Another secret society flourished in small Michigan towns—the Ku Klux
Klan. After his death, my aunt was going through some of her father's things
packed in a trunk. At the bottom was a white hooded robe. This discovery
appalled my aunt, and my mother when she heard of it. They couldn't imagine their gregarious, civic-minded father associated with the KKK. Dan Cole
seemed to have an affinity for secret, all-male societies.

Like his older brother, Dan embraced civic duty with gusto. He was
credited with guiding the Walkerville Bank, a branch of the Scottville Bank
(owned by C.W. McPhail) through the 1929 Stock Market Crash and
Depression and keeping the bank solvent. He served on the board of education, as mayor of the village, and as the clerk at all farm auctions. The image
of him hanging up his suit coat and pulling a white robe over his head is a
disturbing one.

# 1999

I envy Sarah her attachment to Pelican, arriving at the age of 26 and leaving
it—and the world—on her way to a wedding when she was 77. All her adult
life, she was connected to one town, with two brief moves, but she always
returned to Pelican. However, her children, except Tillie, moved away. (Later,
even Tillie left Pelican. As an adult, she relocated to Denver.) Sarah's young-

est, my grandfather, settled in western Michigan in a town smaller than Pelican. This town became my touchstone; it is my home, a mythic home, a place where I will never live again, yet it's where I say I'm from when people ask.

My grandfather, Daniel Cole, became a banker in Walkerville, Michigan, working at a branch of the bank his older brother worked for. Walkerville is my Lake Wobegon. I moved from there when I was eight, but a hundred strands still connect me to the town. Both parents and their parents were Walkerville inhabitants, and my childhood memories are housed there. I often wonder what kind of person I would be today if I had never left, if I had stayed.

That desire of being rooted in the Midwest brought me back after thirty-two years away, years in which I'd attended college, lived in West Africa as a Peace Corps Volunteer, and "settled" in Pennsylvania with a marriage and work. When I returned to Michigan, it wasn't to Walkerville, but two hundred miles north. In my sporadic return visits to Walkerville, the town had shrunk and lost its Mayberry glow. Old buildings had been torn down; the new structures were characterless and dull—as charming as pole barns. My grandfather's bank still stood, its stone work obliterated by renovations. His house had been torn down. Gone were his famous flower garden and tennis court.

This ten-acre parcel in northern Michigan is our homestead. We're following a long line of displacers. We have usurped the space where deer browsed; where porcupine, black squirrel, and skunk dug, bred, and ate. We also displaced the hunters who used to track deer and bear. There is resentment from long-time residents toward the newcomers who buy up old farmsteads and hunting land. But their ancestors displaced the Odawa and Ojibway. I sympathize with them, to a degree. I feel regret each time a house goes up in what was an open field. An open field beckons the eye to follow the rise and fall of the land; a field with a house in it stops the eye and announces an end to wandering.

As I plant iris bulbs and Norm builds a stone wall, I wonder what this acreage will look like in a hundred years. Will our house still be here? What will the land look like? Will the conservancy easement agreement, with its perpetuity clause, hold?

# A PROGRESSIVE WORLD

## 1889–1902

*And so we worked until we had a fine farm and a nice home, with nothing to regret in our pioneer experiences. This country proved a fine place for settlers and is now a prosperous farming country with many fine, fine homes and modern facilities for work, as well as schools and churches, railroads, automobiles, etc.*

*Our children have now taken our place in the busy, progressive world. We sold our farm, and with the proceeds, after a trip to the Pacific coast, purchased a small house in town where we can take life easier than on the farm and be near our neighbors. In 1878 another daughter was added to our family circle, and in 1889 a son, who was very much welcomed by us all, and who we thought would be a "child in our old age." But he is now married and has followed his brother in the banking business in Michigan. The younger daughter married well and is busy with her fine family of five children, and the older daughter is a government clerk at Washington. We are 'seventy years young' in good health and still looking forward to 'old age' with our grandchildren. We feel that our lives have not been altogether in vain. Of course every life has its bitter and sweet experiences, but on the whole ours has been a happy one. If we have missed some of the advantages and excitement of city life, we certainly have had compensation in the simplicity, purity and wholesomeness of a country life with the purpose of founding a home, rearing our children as well as we were able, and serving the community in which we lived in our humble way, and have had a greater measure of happiness and content than many who have acquired great riches.*

—Sarah Moore Leonard Cole
(Pseud.) Country Teacher

When Sarah was forty-four, she gave birth to Daniel Shell Cole, my grandfather. In one of the many letters between Sarah and Georgina, who was nineteen when her youngest brother was born, Sarah assures her daughter on April 24, 1889, that "I am improving nicely today. Have had lots of callers—the baby is quite a wonder." Georgina was apparently living in the Seattle area at this time. Her mother asks Georgie to bring the incubator as freight, reminding her that she is entitled to one hundred pounds. The intended use for the incubator is not known. Sarah goes on to say that the baby "is just as nice & fat as a butterball & sleeps all the time nearly. He is just as good as he can be—strong and hearty." She comments that the "little shirts and night-dresses are too small." She lists the spring jobs, including the fixing of the sheep pasture fence, and mentions that "Papa has to go collecting delinquent taxes now."

These letters to her daughter reveal a rather tired, frazzled Sarah. A letter on May 19, 1889, gives a flavor of the Coles' domestic life.

*My Dear Georgie*

*We looked for a letter from you last night but were disappointed. I will write you a few lines any way for I know it will be welcome to you. I have just put baby Danie [sic] off into papa's arms. I don't know how long he will be able to keep him. I write expecting to jump any minute—baby takes more tending than any of the others. I think it is because he is so badly tonguetied that he takes in wind as he nurses for I notice he cannot keep his hold good. I will have it clipped the first time I take him to town. We have got the carriage of Mrs. Carr. Tillie brought it up yesterday—when it is repainted & newly upholstered it will be nearly as good as it ever was. Cost $5. & papa thinks it a good bargain. Everything at home has to take its time & moves slowly. I have my work table & it is a daisy. We painted it with paint left from the house—olive cream. We have not yet got the carpet off but hope to this week & then I am going to put in one day visiting each week. Sure almost everyone than ever came to see me has been here since baby was born & I am really hungry to get out. My help is a real blessing if she will only stay with me but she certainly has a weakness for all the old baches & widowers.*

*Tues. 21 I stopped to see Aunt Lib (she has not been over since the baby was born). She & Uncle Will & Gert & Bert came over & since Tillie has had one of her old attacks of pleurisy, so I could not get a minute to write. Baby takes lots of tending is troubled with wind. I think it is because he is so tonguetied he can't keep a tight hold to nurse. I forgot I wrote this before.*

Sarah drew lines through two sentences near the end when she realized she was repeating herself. Aunt Lib was Mary Elizabeth Cady Cole and Uncle Will was William Henry Cole, companions on the 1871 emigration. "Clipping" was the remedy for freeing the baby's tongue, held down to the floor of the mouth by an extra membrane.

Later on October 29, 1889, George wrote to his daughter. He seems to be reassuring her that she has not been slighted. Letters played a crucial role in keeping the family intact while they were separated geographically.

*We are all well Mamma is not very strong, the baby is quite a tax on her constitution but I think she will be all right again as soon as baby is weaned. Now Georgie I write this letter to let you understand that I have by no means forgotten you.*

Georgina moved around, taking jobs on the west coast, in Washington state, and later in Washington, D.C. When Evander was killed in 1919, she came for the funeral from her home in Charleston, West Virginia, according to the local newspaper obituary.

In a letter dated January 12, 1890, Sarah tells her daughter that "I am trying every day to make him say Georgie." Her letters to Georgie reveal the everyday Sarah, the concerned parent and sustainer of family connections. Dannie was doted on, a precious life that everyone in the family coddled. In another letter on May 18, 1891, apparently to Georgie, Sarah writes:

*I wish you could see Dannie he is so brown & rosy. A few days ago he found some big white squash seeds by Peggy. She was lying in the grass by the fence & he picked one up in each hand & called to me 'Peggy laid a weggs' kept repeating it till I went to see & how I laughed at dinner. I told him to tell papa what he found out there & he looked as excited & said 'found Peggy nest—Peggy laid a weggs.' Today he came in with two more squash seeds & said he had found some more Peggy's weggs—they have got spilled when Papa was planting.*

While her two-year-old was a constant source of joy, she was upset about her older son's (Evander or "Bud") attachment to a young woman. A section on the other side of this letter, which someone has crossed out with blue pencil, indicates a fiercer, disapproving streak.

> *Bud went up to Klugg's fishing Sat. evening & came back Sunday eve. Caught 40 bass. Brought 9 home & today we have dined on baked fish. He will probably tell you how he went over to Barnesville to hear Mrs. George's concert last week.*
>
> *Georgie he's stuck to Gert Crandall again. I just pray she will dosomething that will disgust him with her forever but I don't believe she can. He seems to show sense in every other place but ...*

Was Bud aware of his mother's disapproval? Most likely. Sarah made her judgments known. My Aunt Beth recalls an incident from her girlhood while eating at Grandma Cole's. Cousin Louise, one of Tillie's daughters, came downstairs wearing anklets, and Sarah commented on them as inappropriate. Anklets were a daring fashion statement compared to the long cotton stockings that most women and girls wore.

In these letters to Georgie, rules of punctuation are thrown by the wayside. Sarah often uses dashes rather than periods, if she places any end punctuation. The first word in sentences are not capitalized. Her schoolteacher persona is absent. A subsequent letter is dated April 31st, then crossed out and corrected with May 1st, 1892. This one is crammed with family and local news. The sentences wind around the margins and fill every available space.

> *My Dear Georgie*
>
> *I have just rocked Dannie to sleep & now can expect a few quiet moments to write to you. Tillie has started going to church & S.S. regular. ... She went in spite of bad weather today & has stayed to take part in a S.S. concert. I don't know whether she will get home tonight or not. Bud has not put in an appearance today & I have felt a little lonely as the weather is raw & uncomfortable ...*

Sarah's letters are conversations and at times Georgie seems more a peer than a daughter. She says that "Dannie's shoes were all right. The souvenirs from the Expo. ground are quite precious." She gives more news about Dannie's interaction with the natural world when she tells Georgie that Dan is in terror of the old gobbler & holds his breath every time he gets frightened.

Around the perimeter of the page, Sarah writes of her sale of a dollar's worth of roses and of her purchase of "20 varieties of tea roses (5¢ a piece). They are nicely rooted & will bloom this summer. All colors ever heard of ..."

On April 20, 1892, Sarah was forty-seven years old. She writes to Georgie that the night before she and "papa" had gone to town in their new buggy, and that she is "lame and sore every inch" from painting in the house. In a May 27 letter, she reports that there were no apple blossoms yet. Like many of Sarah's letters, someone has cut out sections of it. The remaining portion gives a glimpse of the domestic quality of life on the farm:

> ... carpet down this forenoon & now we have only the kitchen & cellar left & hope to finish tomorrow. ... & have everything lovely for Sunday. We have the front yard quite clean but the back is yet to do. We enjoy working at it evenings papa & all. We made a great bonfire with the Christmas tree (fir) on top the other night. Tillie shouted & hollered & so did Dan ...

There are a few more words, including missing you. The bond between Sarah and the daughter who had been with her on the trip to Minnesota was strong. Their letters eased the separation.

After thirty years of farming near Prairie Lake, Sarah and George sold the farm in 1901 and moved to Seattle with Dan, the only child still at home. This migration was most likely by train. Although a greater distance, it was less arduous than their wagon trip in 1871. George's obituary reports that he had become somewhat discouraged with farming on account of ill health. They stayed less than a year in Seattle with Georgie, who had moved there earlier. Georgie's letter to Tillie, who had her own household in Pelican, provides a flavor of the Seattle months. This letter is typed on stationery from the Piano Warerooms of the Ramaker Music Co. Georgie was more conversant with modern conveniences—the typewriter and telephone—than the folks back in Pelican.

*July 16, 1902*

*Dear Tillie:—*

*I have been having so much dissipation I don't know whether I can collect my wits to write or not. It seems as if all good things come in a bunch. Monday night I went home with tickets for a fine concert in the Grand Opera House, and full freedom to spend the next day at Snoqualmie Falls. Well, we did some good hustling, I tell you, in order to take advantage of it all. Mamma had washed during the forenoon, and in the afternoon went down town with papa to attend to some business, and then after supper she and I and Dan went to the concert. It was quite good, and I will send you a program, but we did not get home till after twelve o'clock, and then only slept till five as we had to get up and get ready to go on the excursion to the Falls, which left Seattle at nine. Only mamma and I went, as Dan is so interested in his job at the grocery that he didn't even mention going …*

Georgie's upfront announcement of her dissipation probably referred to a stomach or intestinal problem. It had nothing to do with alcohol, as the Coles were not ones to indulge. The whole family kept close tabs on Dan's development as an infant, and this continued as he entered his early teens. Georgie, and Evander too, were making sure their much younger brother cultivated a serious attitude toward work, although as she observes, the West Coast attitude was much more easygoing. The letter continues:

*He is as sober and business-like as an owl about his work, and as I was watching him dust this morning, as I was waiting in the store for the car, I couldn't help thinking how he used to go around with a rag when he was about two years old, and help mama 'bush 'e dust' as he used to say, and I wondered what we would have thought to look forward to him now. When he was weighing something he pursed out his lips just as he used to when he was writing when he went to school to me the first time …*

*I forgot to tell you that Dan answers the telephone in the store, and so is getting some good practice in that line. He telephoned down to me one day, as nice as you please. Mr. P. goes off and leaves him in charge while he comes down to the city to order goods, and seems to trust him a good deal. I wonder what people in P.R. would think of doing such a thing as that. But that is the way everything goes here. It seems as if people leave so much in the hands of their helpers, whoever they are, and do anything to get free from the work themselves. No one seems to work very hard here. No one, or at least very few, are rich, and yet everyone seems to have plenty of money to do what they want to with.*

*I must close now, as I am getting such a sick-headache I can hardly write.*

*I guess I shall have to be more quiet for a while.*

*With much love to you all, I remain,*

*Yours as ever,*
GEORGIE

Dan spent that summer in Seattle working hard, with progress reports going back to Tillie in Pelican Rapids.

*Dan is like Bud, I can see more and more. It would surprise you to see how important and business like he is when waiting on customers. He never can learn to hurry, but he works steadily, and I guess Mr. Phalen is pretty well satisfied with him. Mr. P. was off on a toot Sunday night Dan thought, at least he didn't come in Monday morning until very late, but sent a boy to help Dan, and left him in full charge. Dan thought he was overworked, but got along all right. The store is fully as large as Carr's old store, where Mills was, so you see he has a good deal of responsibility, as he had to take orders and put them up between times of waiting on customers that came in, and get ready to deliver in the afternoon. He works in the store mornings, and spends nearly all the afternoon delivering ...*

In another letter to Tillie on Sept. 1, 1902, Georgie writes of "a severe spell of homesickness to contend with." She carried the weight of each family member's trouble.

*Papa has been sick, and Dan proved unable to do all the work needed at the grocery, so had to give way for a young man of seventeen which was not at all to his discredit as the grocer told a neighbor that Dan was the best boy he ever had, but he must have someone who could lift the heavy sacks of flour and feed, and papa objected to Dan's doing that. However of course he couldn't help feeling uneasy for a while, but not for long, as the other grocer offered him a job so that he has had work nearly all the while up to school time, which began this morning. The last man he worked for praised him up to papa too, and really it surprises us all to see how he takes hold of things ... We had a great day yesterday. Went to church, Dan went to S.S. decided on the minute when we got home to go and see the bat-tle-ships at Bremerton, as we saw in the paper that there were four of them there just now, besides two torpedo boats and two training ships for the sailors. We took the trip without a set-back, and will describe it to you sometime ...*

Georgie seems to be taken with the more casual, artistic lifestyle of Washington state. All social customs are measured against those of Pelican Rapids. However, Sarah is not as enthusiastic, as indicated in the next section of the letter, written on Sept. 3.

*People go to each others' houses to spend the evening, etc., but I hardly ever hear of such a thing as their taking meals together ... our neighbors run about to each others' gates and gardens and visit any old time with kitchen aprons and sunbon-nets or whatever else they happen to have on, and do not seem to be either slouchy or too particular. Our nearest neighbor on one side teaches the primary room at Columbia and her husband is an artist in an engraving firm down here in Seattle. Next to her lives a lady who paints pictures that are quite noted here, besides doing her own work. Next are an old couple who are just living cosily the rest of their lives and not trying to work. He is seventy and she not much behind although she declares she never got beyond twenty-two. She has pretty white hair and dresses in pink, white, and lavender waists and ribbons, and it does not look out of place either. Next are two German families with a good many children, but just as jolly and kind as can be. I won't tire you by telling any more, but I thought I would give you an idea of who mama can spend her time with. She need not be lonesome if she could only make herself interested in these people, for they are just as friendly as can be, and good company. I like the neighborhood very much.*

The homesickness referred to earlier may have been Sarah's. After thirty years in Pelican, this move to Seattle could have been too big of an adjust-ment. They returned "home" and bought a house in the village.

# A BETTER COUNTRY

**R**etired from farming and now living in town, Sarah and George moved to a different rhythm. George took on the offices of town constable and deputy sheriff. The ill health that caused him to sell the farm by Prairie Lake continued in his new location. His 1927 obituary tells how the Minnesota winters took a toll on George Cole.

> *Mr. Cole has been a semi-invalid for over 25 years, due to rheumatism contracted from long drives and exposure in severe winter weather, incidental to his work as deputy sheriff under Mr. A. Brandenburg, sheriff of this county years ago. His last illness was of but 8 days duration and his mind was alert and his faculties keen almost to the last. Death came as the result of uremic poisoning and complications due to old age.*

Bad health and financial difficulties, too. There is the earlier mention of George withdrawing his membership from the Masonic Lodge; and in a December 18, 1917, letter to Dan, who was then in Walkerville, Michigan, he urgently requests money: "I am in need of more money can you respond to the call send $50. or $75. as soon as possible." Perhaps his banker son was watching over his father's funds, but that isn't implied by the tone. He was asking his son for money.

The short relocation to Scottville, Michigan, may have been spurred by low funds. In 1919, Evander had a bungalow built for his parents, but they stayed only a few months. They had just returned to Pelican when they were informed of Evander's death, near Munising in the Upper Peninsula. They built a "modern" house, their final home, near Tillie's, on the east side of the village. Sarah was within a short distance of her grandchildren, Tillie's children.

After Sarah's death in 1922, George lived with Georgie, who was again living in Pelican. The eldest child was drawn back periodically to home base, but apparently the area didn't supply her with a livelihood. She moved around the country, working at a variety of jobs on both coasts, and when she married, her husband's employment with Standard Oil took them to Bismarck, North Dakota.

I have my great-aunt Georgie to thank for what I know of the 1871 emigration. I had always assumed Sarah took the initiative in getting the narrative published, until I came across a 1915 letter to Dan and his wife.

*Washington, D.C., March 21, 1915*

*My dear Dan and Grace:*

*This isn't going to be much of a letter, but just want to say 'Hello' and send you a copy of something of which I am very proud. Mama has written up her pioneer experiences for me, and I have copied it to send to the "Farmers Despatch" [sic] of St. Paul, for I think they will be glad to get it to publish, as they are calling for stories along that line, and I got mama to promise when I was home last fall that she would write this up and I would type it and see whether they would publish it. Anyway we will have it to keep, and that is worth a good deal. If you think of it, when Evander goes over there, you let him read it; but unless we get it published I am not going to send him a copy until I get time to make some more, if I ever do.*

*I hope you will think enough of this to take good care of it, and write me whether you received it and what you think of it. I want you to keep it if you care for it, but if you don't, just send it back to me. Don't let it go out of your hands to anyone else.*

*The last page was just the way mama wrote it first, but afterward she thought she wanted to end it as it is on next to the last page, so I copied them both for our benefit, but the next to the last page is the way it goes to the Farmers Despatch [sic] ...*

Georgie goes on with more family news. The letter is typewritten, except for the sentence "Don't let it go out of your hands to anyone else," which was added in later by hand. Georgina was aware of the value of this record and made sure her siblings were impressed with the family treasure they had. The last page, not included in the newspaper account, presents Sarah's "bittersweet" perspective. This was before Evander's death.

128

*We are not longer young. Our four children have taken our place in the busy, progressive world. They are an honor to us, and we feel that our lives have not been altogether in vain. Of course every life has to have bitter and sweet experiences, but on the whole ours has been a happy and busy one.*

*The panorama changes. Few of our old-time settlers remain. Many have passed on to the 'better country' we all hope to reach at last, and others are scattered to the four winds of the earth. We have a special love for and interest in our old-time pioneer friends, and I will record a few names that I would rejoice to meet, here or in the hereafter: Tuttle, Harris, Blyberg, Blodgett, Lacy, Everhart, Burdick, Dunn, and of course the Leonards, and the Coles.*

I think Sarah and Georgina and Tillie would be happy with my interest, would be glad that their words have been passed on to me. Where I'd like to leave them is on the lawn in Pelican Rapids in 1918, a few months before the end of World War I. There is a big family gathering for Sarah and George's fiftieth wedding anniversary. All of the children are there, as well as six grandchildren. Will Harris, Georgina's husband, is not in the picture. Perhaps he is the photographer. Basswood leaves are pinned to their chests, emblems of the trees that had provided them with their first home near Prairie Lake back in 1871.

I've followed Sarah to find my place in the circle, to discover that just by being born, without any effort on my part, I am automatically a link in history. I can only hope my nieces and nephew will one day read my words and pass them on, along with Sarah and Georgina and Tillie's. The three generations of Coles I encountered on this trip have all long ago emigrated to "a better country." One day I will follow them on that journey. But their words and pictures have provided me with a way of communicating with them and interacting with their lives. I can only hope to leave behind a legacy as valuable.

# ABOUT THE AUTHOR

Marla Kay Houghteling spent the first eight years of her life in Walkerville, Michigan. Having lived in Florida, Illinois, West Africa and Pennsylvania, she returned to Michigan and settled in Harbor Springs. She has written two books of poems: *The Blue House* and *Assisted Living*. Under a grant from MCACA, she wrote an historical novel, *The Journey of Aurora Starr*.

# Endnotes

1   Derleth, *The Wisconsin*, 184.

2   Note from Beth Cole Swanson.

3   Derleth, *The Wisconsin*, 188.

4.  Derleth, *The Wisconsin*, 186–87.

5   Derleth, *The Wisconsin*, 188.

6   Eberlein, *Juneau County*, 47.

7   Legler, *Wisconsin History*, 283.

8   Eberlein, *Juneau County*, 10.

9   Eberlein, *Juneau County*, 160.

10  Compton's.

11  Folwell, *History of Minnesota*, 480n.

12  Van Cleve, "Reminiscence of Ft. Snelling," 81.

13  Ourada, *Menominee*.

14  Gilman, *Red River Trails*, 87.

15  Gilman, *Red River Trails*, 86.

16  Gilman, *Red River Trails*, 81.

17  Folwell, *History of Minnesota*, 61.

18  Gilman, *Red River Trails*, v.

19  Gilman, *Red River Trails*, 73.

20  Gilman, *Red River Trails*, 24.

21  Folwell, *History of Minnesota*, 362.

22  Pelican Centennial Committee, *Century at Rapids*, 11.

23  Pelican Centennial Committee, *Century at Rapids*, 11.

24  Qtd. in Folwell, *History of Minnesota*, 96.

25  Pelican, 40.

26  www.chicagotribune.com/history/great-chicago-fire.

27  www.hon-area.org/history.html#barrett.

28    Pelican Centennial Committee, *Century at Rapids*, 56.

29    Kelly, *My Captivity*.

30    "Brown County."

31    Folwell, *History of Minnesota*, 22, 23.

32    Tanner, *Ojibwa*.

33    Eberlein, *Juneau County*, 5.

34    Eberlein, *Juneau County*, 5.

35    Pelican, 10.

36    Tanner, *Ojibwa*.

# Bibliography

"Brown County and the Sioux Massacre." 7 Mar. 1997. 2 Oct. 1999. http://www.ic.new-ulm.mn.us/tour/dakota.html.

*Compton's Reference Collection 1996.* CD-ROM. Compton's NewMedia, Inc., 1995.

Derleth, August. *The Wisconsin, River of a Thousand Isles.* New York and Toronto: Farrar & Rinehart, Inc., 1942. 184–88.

Eberlein, Merton, ed. *Juneau County, The First Hundred Years.* Friendship: Juneau County Historical Society and New Past Press Inc., 1988.

Folwell, William Watts. *A History of Minnesota, Vol. III.* St. Paul: Minnesota Historical Society, 1969.

Gilman, Rhoda R., Carolyn Gilman and Deborah M. Stultz. *The Red River Trails, Oxcart Routes Between St. Paul and the Selkirk Settlement 1820–1870.* St. Paul: Minnesota Historical Society, 1979.

Kelly, Fanny. *Narrative of My Captivity Among the Sioux Indians.* Clark and Mary Lee Spence (ed.). Chicago: Lakeside Press, R.R. Donnelley & Sons Co., 1990. xxxi.

Legler, Henry E. *Leading Events of Wisconsin History–The Story of the State.* Milwaukee: The Sentinel Co., 1901.

Mackey, Albert Gallatin. *The History of Freemasonry–Its Legendary Origins.* New York and Avenel: Gramercy Books (Random House Value Publishing, Inc.), 1996.

Ourada, Patricia K. *The Menominee.* New York and Philadelphia: Chelsea House, 1990.

Pelican Rapids Centennial Committee. *A Century at the Rapids.* Josten's American Yearbook Co., 1983.

Scacheri, Mario and Mabel. *Winnebago Boy.* New York: Harcourt, Brace and Co., 1937.

*75 Years of Progress 1883–1958* (Pelican Rapids Diamond Jubilee June 22–24).

Tanner, Helen Hornbeck. *The Ojibwa* (Indians of North America series). New York and Philadelphia: Chelsea House Publishers, 1992.

Van Cleve, Charlotte O. "A Reminiscence of Ft. Snelling." *Minnesota Historical Society Collections 1870–80*. St. Paul: Minnesota Historical Society, 1880. 76–81.

Zinn, Howard. *A People's History of the United States*. New York: Harper Perennial-HarperCollins, 1980. 206–46.

# *Acknowledgments*

My thanks to:

*In Wisconsin—*
Merton Eberlein, who generously shared his knowledge and memories.
Cynthe Sundin, who lent me a copy of *Juneau County: The First Hundred Years.*
James L. Hansen and Geraldine Strey of the State Historical Society of Wisconsin for their prompt and courteous answers to all my questions.

*In Minnesota—*
Minnesota Historical Society for locating the newspaper containing Sarah's account.
Mildred Frazee, my gracious Pelican contact.
The town of Pelican Rapids, Minnesota, for its existence and hospitality.

*In Michigan—*
My mother, Kathleen Cole Houghteling, and my aunts, Ruth Cole Raby and Beth Cole Swanson, for all those letters, photos, and stories.
Writers North!, whose spirit, support and even opinions, are appreciated. Helen Leithauser for her careful reading and notations on the beginning portions.

*And—*
The Ragdale Foundation for a room of my own and dinner at 6:30.

Made in the USA
Middletown, DE
07 October 2022